The Nationalization of State Government

The Nationalization of State Government

Edited by
Jerome J. Hanus
The American University

LexingtonBooks
D.C. Heath and Company
Lexington, Massachusetts
Toronto

Library of Congress Cataloging in Publication Data

Main entry under title:

The Nationalization of state government.

1. Federal government—United States—Addresses, essays, lectures.
2. Grants-in-aid—United States—Addresses, essays, lectures. 3. Inter-
governmental fiscal relations—United States—Addresses, essays, lectures.
I. Hanus, Jerome J.
JK325.N28   353.9'292   80-8635
ISBN 0-669-04334-6

Copyright © 1981 by D.C. Heath and Company

Published simultaneously in Canada

Printed in the United States of America

International Standard Book Number: 0-669-04334-6

Library of Congress Catalog Card Number: 80-8635

Contents

List of Figures
and Tables

Introduction

The chapters in this book have a common concern with the political impact of federal grant-in-aid policies on state and national policymaking. The heart of their concern is with the continuing health of an operating representative democracy designed originally to attain both the "general welfare" and limited government. That the first goal is still sought after 200 years would not come as a surprise to either the Framers or to students of history. But that so many intellectuals and politicians today believe there is no need to concern ourselves with having a "limited" government is indeed astonishing to anyone who has looked at the extent to which the growth in government activities has impaired the liberty of many institutions and citizens. A government "doing good" has its costs if we but look for them.

Much of the political commentary of the last 40 years has tended to denigrate the institutional mechanisms created by the Framers to check national power. An uncomfortably recent example of this was the literature encouraging the accumulation of power by the presidency and urging chief executives to use this power energetically and continuously. The unstated assumption was that such power would only be used wisely and well. Vietnam and Watergate, however, put a severe crimp in this presumption and stimulated fresh appraisals of the continuing validity of the constitutional structure. Books by Philip Kurland and Archibald Cox come immediately to mind as representative of this trend. In addition, nowhere was this more evident than in a renewed appreciation of the separation of powers principle, implicit in the Constitution, which was reflected in the reassertion of congressional power in the 1970s.

Strong presidential leadership was being demanded in the 1930s, and this coincided with a demand by a majority of voters for the federal government to assume responsibilities for smoothing out the business cycle and to perform a number of national police powers superseding those traditionally performed by state and local governments. Both demands assumed the inherent superiority of national-government authority over the private economic sector and over "parochial" local governments. The Constitution implied, although it did not require, the existence of a private economic sector from which would emanate individual and group interests, none of which would dominate the national government because of the existence of a bicameral Congress, the separation of powers principle, and the innovative principle of federalism. The last principle was expected to check national governmental control because it was assumed that national government would be authorized to perform only a few functions. In addition, self-reliant citizens would be their own check on imperialist-minded local and state governments.

Conditions were ripe for a strong, pervasive national government from the 1930s on because it was generally felt that only such a government could deal with a national economic depression, a national Cold War, and a national civil rights movement. Much of this was reflected also in a transformed political ideology. Complex market relationships in the private sector driven by a "profit motive" were accused of selfish immorality and class oppression. A central authority was increasingly urged to allocate resources for ensuring economic growth and a "fair" allocation of benefits, if not the burdens.

By the 1970s, these demands for a centralized government were largely fulfilled, although more so in some areas than in others. Federal regulation of much of the economic sector occurred first, but the assumption of state police powers lagged behind only briefly. This was justified partly on the grounds that all parts of the economy were now inextricably bound up with one another, and a new interpretation of individual rights was constructed from the Fourteenth Amendment, which called for their standardization throughout the nation. This latter development was not considered to be regulatory because the protection and fostering of individual rights did not, allegedly, impose any costs on individuals.

Because some of these interests could not constitutionally be attained by direct federal legislation, resort was increasingly made to the mechanism of federal grants-in-aid. This was often referred to as "cooperative federalism," "picket-fence federalism," and other synonyms, but references always avoided the phrase "dual sovereignty," which was considered an anachronism. These intergovernmental programs now number almost 500 and take differing forms depending on their degree of specificity and the number of federal requirements accompanying them. The pervasiveness of the federal regulations accompanying these grants today blankets state and local governments and imposes delays and reporting costs analogous to those found in the marketplace. Whether the costs are too high with respect to the benefits of the programs is, and will remain, a matter of dispute.

The chapters that follow take a closer look at what has occurred and is occurring in this dynamic area of intergovernmental relations. Much of the change in constitutional relationships unfortunately has escaped the public's attention. Rhetoric about policies of new federalism and decentralization has disguised the reality that our government is becoming more monocentric than most people realize. This has led, as Professor Zimmerman observes in chapter 3, to a federal role that "has produced a reallocation of political power between state and local chief executives and their respective legislative bodies and has changed significantly the lobbying activities of private and public interest groups by shifting many of their activities to Washington, D.C."

Academicians studying intergovernmental relations and observing this trend have seen no dangers in it. "Cooperative federalism" has a reassuring sound to it, as though there were merely a mutual accommodation of interests, such as when two parties enter into a contract. When writers do acknowledge the seeming stringency of multitudinous regulations accompanying the grants-in-aid, the regulations are dismissed all too frequently as legalisms that can be avoided by a political bargaining process in which state officials sometimes gain the upper hand (capture the federal agency?) and federal officials sometimes do. In any case, the legal requirements are assumed to be largely irrelevant.

Much of the literature confirms that this kind of behavior and these kinds of rationalizations do indeed occur. Here only a few observations need be made. First, the attitude that laws or regulations may be side-stepped, broken, or ignored as long as the "parties get on with the job" is one that should not be encouraged if one desires a "government of laws and not of men." While it is exceedingly difficult to validate empirically, a familiarity with history, especially political biography, suggests that a spillover effect from one policy area to another does occur. One of the unfortunate characteristics of the 1960s and 1970s was (and is) the uncritical acceptance of the slogan "beat the system" (that is, "beat the law"). Like "rules were made to be broken" (originally directed toward anachronistic laws that a legislature simply had not gotten around to repealing), such an attitude encourages cynicism toward all authority.

Second, the primacy of bargaining in which one party occasionally gets the upper hand and sometimes the other does, leads to the dissolution of all vestiges of accountability. Who is the citizen to blame when a grant-in-aid program appears to be foolish or to have counterproductive consequences? To whom does the irate citizen complain if not to the agency with ultimate legal authority? If a federal agency has final legal authority but that authority has been informally bargained away, then of what good to citizens are constitutional theories of accountability? Even citizen-participation requirements can have the effect of further blurring this chain of accountability—thus making a bad situation worse.

Third, a common reaction to evidence of the unmanageability of intergovernmental programs is to "streamline" federal agencies and their procedures. Unified auditing systems, federal coordinating committees, and designation of lead agencies are among the recommendations frequently made. While modification in procedures can sometimes reduce waste and delay, it does not directly address the political costs involved, nor even the wasted fiscal resources as every potential grant recipient tries to get a "piece of the action" irrespective of whether the funds will actually further the purposes of the grant or not.

In chapter 5, Colella and Beam, summarizing the studies by the Advisory Commission on Intergovernmental Relations, emphasize the congressional committee structure, which effectively precludes evaluative oversight of grants-in-aid. Congressmen see the continuation of grants-in-aid going to their constituents as an important element in their reelection efforts and therefore are unlikely to want them threatened by objective evaluations. This chapter suggests that sweeping generalizations about national policy-making must be forgone in favor of more detailed analyses on a program-by-program basis.

Chapters 1 and 2 engage in specific analyses of the requirements accompanying several intergovernmental programs to illustrate the transformation of federal-state relations from one of federal subvention of state and local activities to federal dominance through a variety of administrative techniques. In chapter 1, Hanus argues that writers have overlooked and therefore underestimated the degree to which federal officials control the state's decision-making structure through their regulatory requirements. He recommends that program evaluations undertaken should include explicit political concepts, in this case "authority costs." These, in addition to traditional fiscal costs, would give a much deeper and more realistic picture of what has been happening over the last 15 years in intergovernmental relations.

In chapter 2, Dubnick and Gitelson describe the nationalizing mechanisms at work and offer a classificatory scheme for comprehending their impact on the political system. They find that the recent nationalization of authority has accompanied implementation procedures intended to decentralize policy administration and that this approach works better with some types of programs than with others.

In chapter 3, Zimmerman describes how partial preemption has taken place and illustrates the process by examining the air-pollution problem in the United States. In so doing he notes the accompanying shift in power relationships at the state level, the incomprehensibility to the citizen of this complex set of relationships, and the concomitant frustration of national objectives.

In chapter 4, Jones examines the policy arguments that have been made for and against federal regulation of schools. He finds a discrepancy between what public opinion supports and what the federal government demands (for example, in busing for racial balance), with the result that in some parts of the nation there has been a massive desertion of public schools. After examining the role that interest groups play, he considers alternatives to such regulation and estimates their respective consequences. His chapter offers a good example of the need for a precise definition of the goals sought by a government policy.

One hopes that the perspectives offered in this book will lead researchers and policymakers to take a renewed interest in federal-state relations. Absurdities in the system—such as it is—are not the only causes of citizen disenchantment with government, state or federal, but they do contribute to that disenchantment and consequently to the health of our constitutional democracy. If, after looking at what has occurred, one decides that our federal system is outmoded, then this conclusion should be faced squarely and a public decision to that effect should be made. Such a decision should not be made by an accumulation of haphazard unconsidered policies taken without reference to what is happening to our constitutional framework. If little else, this book emphasizes that a gaping hole in the research on the subject is the lack of criteria for determining when a "national" need exists that requires a national response and when such a need exists that can be responded to differentially by subnational governments. Such work would go a long way toward giving policymakers the kind of intellectual weaponry needed to offset importunities of interest groups. It might even lead them to conclude that the need could be best resolved over time if left to the social dynamics of each community.

Acknowledgements

The editor is grateful to the Southern Growth Policies Board, especially to its executive director, E. Blaine Liner, and to the National Science Foundation for supporting the writing and editing of this book. Special thanks must be given to Harriette Hawkins, who worked as research assistant during the project and made an invaluable contribution to the editing process, and to Lou Phillips, who offered her splendid services as a typist and a coordinator of the drafts of the chapters. Only through her efficiency did the project remain on schedule.

The Nationalization of State Government

1 Authority Costs in Intergovernmental Relations

Jerome J. Hanus

The issue of government regulation was one of the distinguishing characteristics of the 1970s, and it bids well to be one for the 1980s. While the content of the debate is most notably characterized by legislation calling for deregulation of the transportation and petroleum industries, it also includes legislative measures providing for congressional vetoes of federal regulations, a balanced national budget, increased public participation in the regulatory process, and funding for litigation costs for parties substantially prevailing in civil suits against regulatory agencies.

Inherent in the controversy over these regulatory issues is a concern that excessive or inappropriate regulation has inhibited productivity and has imposed excessive costs on the business economy of the nation. Associated with this concern, and identified especially with free-market economists such as Milton Friedman, William Simon, and Murray Weidenbaum, is a fear that a heavily regulated economy means decreasing freedom in other areas.[1] For example, extensive regulation of education is said to decrease the freedom of individuals to choose the type and content of education they desire. As regulatory activity becomes more pervasive, it is likely, it is alleged, to lead to an excessively dependent citizenry, one that finds itself confined by the same regulations that protect and subsidize it.

As interesting and significant as this debate is, another more complex and esoteric controversy also has emerged. This is the degree of freedom from federal control that state governments should be able to exercise. Unlike the debate over business regulation, the character and ramifications of intergovernmental regulation have not been clarified by legislation. Bills to consolidate categorical grants, to designate lead agencies for supervising administrative requirements, or to remove state participation in general revenue sharing are addressed as economy measures, not as regulatory issues. Grants-in-aid are still perceived to be assistance to the "locals" rather than the imposition of costs on some groups for the benefit of others. Whether there are marginal benefits is, of course, a major concern to students of intergovernmental relations, as it is to all students of regulation.[2] Unfortunately, ignored by writers on the subject is the cost to government itself of reduced confidence in it by the citizenry. This type of cost, referred to here as an *authority cost,* is compounded in a federal system of government.[3]

1

Even adoption of the policies of "creative" and "new" federalism has done little to rejuvenate the debate over the legal and administrative integrity of state governments, although it has encouraged writers to reappraise the economic efficiency of intergovernmental grants. However, growing public disenchantment with federal programs and a movement for greater public participation have begun to stimulate a reappraisal of the current relationship between federal and state governments in the hopes of encouraging more interest in subnational policymaking.

Although discussions of federalism take many forms, fiscal and administrative questions have increasingly begun to appear in the literature. In particular, studies of the implementation of federal programs at the local level have attracted considerable attention among policymakers because they have revealed unanticipated costs in such programs.[4] Similar conclusions also have been found in studies of government regulation of business and industry and have led to efforts in Congress and in executive agencies to modify regulations or to reduce government intervention in specific economic sectors.[5]

Many of the economic costs arising from the regulation of business are evident also in federal regulation of state governments.[6] Moreover, just as Milton Friedman has emphasized the political and social costs of government regulation of the private sector in the sense of a diminution of individual freedom, so government regulation of constitutionally prescribed subnational governments carries with it costs in political accountability and in citizen confidence in government institutions. These types of costs, although more amorphous than economic ones, also can lead to reduced freedom. The purpose of this chapter is to describe the process by which federal regulation of the states occurs and to describe how the types of costs, especially authority costs, are imposed.

The Federal-State Regulatory Arena

The issue of federal regulation of subnational governments arises primarily because the United States is constitutionally a federalist nation, secondarily, because of a strong tradition of localism, and finally, because of efficiency arguments. If it were not for the Constitution, the issue of federalism would resolve itself into questions of the continuing relevance of a localist tradition and the marginal costs of nationally administered programs. The last two questions are ones that every nation, whether federalist or unitary, must struggle with. Their resolution depends in large measure on the degree to which direct central government control is resented or welcomed by key groups in society. Two advantages of a unitary form of government are that public debate can be less abstract and government responsibility more easily defined.

However, simply having the *form* of federalism without each sovereign having substantive powers results not only in an additional economic cost, but also in a very real political one. Differential public expectations toward each level of government contribute significantly to the dynamism of a federalist system. However, a citizenry that expects certain public protections and services but does not get them becomes resentful of government in general because the relationship between responsibility and a particular level of government is too diffuse to comprehend. In such a situation, government activity will tend to be denigrated by the public. Nor is it likely that people will assume participation costs, such as voting in subnational elections or interacting with the state bureaucracy on local matters, when it is known that effective decisions can be taken only at the national level or in accordance with conditions imposed at that level. In this situation, a weak and ineffective government will be ignored or treated with ill-concealed impatience by its citizens as their attention is concentrated on the governmental level where it is perceived that effective decision making takes place.

Without pushing this logic ad absurdum, one also may conclude that habitual disrespect toward authority in one political domain is likely to spill over into disrespect for authority in other areas. Cynicism toward one level of government makes it more difficult for other levels to obtain and rely on the presumptive consent of its population and forces them to give more attention to enforcement procedures than would otherwise be necessary. Thus cynicism toward a weak and ignored state government is likely to have a spillover effect of cynicism toward national government, and vice versa.

The issue of federalism is thus raised in its clearest form: Should and does the United States have strong constitutional subnational governments? To answer this requires discussion of three preliminary questions. One, what is the current legal relationship between the federal and state governments? Two, what is the fiscal relationship between the federal and state governments? Three, how and to what extent does the federal government control state governmental functions?

Legal Bases for Federal Mandates

The U.S. Constitution established the framework of a federalist nation but did not clearly demarcate federal and state relations nor their respective relationships to individual citizens. While the Constitution, unlike the Articles of Confederation, authorized the national government to operate directly on the people in specified functional areas, it was unclear that these were to be the only ones. It is this fact of both the federal and state entities governing the same citizen that underlies the complex and frequently confusing relationships between the two sovereigns.

The federal government was given express jurisdiction, for instance, over apportionment of congressional representatives and over the functions listed in Article I, Section 8.[7] Section 10 listed functions that were expressly forbidden to states. Other provisions in the Constitution referred to specific state responsibilities (for example, in presidential elections, law suits, and admission of new states). In addition, apparently for emphasis, the Tenth Amendment was shortly added: "The powers not delegated to the United States by the Constitution nor prohibited by it to the States, are reserved to the States respectively, or to the people." Beyond these matters, however—and even these became opaque as years went by—controversy and uncertainty as to their constitutionality attended federal and state policy initiatives.[8]

However, one principle would have seemed to be incontrovertible. The federal government could not mandate the performance of a function by a state unless the mandate was based on a constitutional provision. The Supreme Court adhered to a fairly literal interpretation of this principle, deviating from it primarily in interstate-commerce cases, until 1937. In that year, the Court began offering extremely expansive definitions of the interstate-commerce clause, the taxing and spending clauses, and provisions of the Fourteenth Amendment.[9] The result was vastly expanded congressional authority to impose federally determined requirements on states, businesses, and other institutions formerly considered to be within the jurisdiction of the fiscal, commercial, and police powers of the states.

The Sixteenth Amendment also was of importance because it allowed the federal government to increase its wealth dramatically, thus providing the financial basis for expensive new national programs. It led, in practice if not design, to federal co-option of financial resources potentially available to the states, but which they could now recoup only by participating in federally funded programs.[10] Two key cases that rationalized federal supersession of state power in areas where the federal government chose to act were *Massachusetts* v. *Mellon* in 1923 and *Steward Machine Co.* v. *Davis* in 1937.[11] The *Mellon* case involved a challenge by the state to the Maternity Act of 1921, which provided for conditional grants to states "to reduce maternal and infant mortality." The state had argued that the use of federal funds drawn from Massachusetts' taxpayers coerced the state into participation in the grant-in-aid program as the only means by which it could benefit from its own tax dollars. The Court rejected the argument, saying merely that the relationship between federal and state governments was a political question and therefore nonjusticiable. Subsequently, other cases have permitted legal action by a state against federal requirements, but the enjoining of grants-in-aid has not been upheld.[12]

In the *Steward Machine Co.* case, the Court upheld the unemployment provisions of the Social Security Act. The Court noted that some of the federal requirements were "designed to give assurance that the state unemployment compensation law shall be one in substance as well as name." One of the provisions of the act required that state funds be paid to the Secretary of the Treasury with subsequent payments to be made to state authorities only upon proper requisition.

Justice Cardozo argued that this plan did not coerce the states in violation of the Tenth Amendment. After drawing attention to the nationwide dimensions of the Depression, he stated: "It is too late today for the argument to be heard with tolerance that in a crisis so extreme the use of the monies of the nation to relieve the unemployed and their dependents is a use for any purposes than the promotion of the general welfare." He then came to grips with the heart of the states' rights arguments:

> The assailants of the statute say that its dominant end and aim is to drive the state legislatures under the whip of economic pressure into the enactment of unemployment compensation laws at the bidding of the central government. Supporters of the statute say that its operation is not constraint, but the creation of a larger freedom, the states and the nation joining in a cooperative endeavor to avert a common evil. . . .

> The Social Security Act is an attempt to find a method by which all these public agencies may work together to a common end. Every dollar of the new taxes will continue in all likelihood to be used and needed by the nation as long as states are unwilling, whether through timidity or for other motives, to do what can be done at home. . . .

> Who then is coerced through the operation of this statute? Not the taxpayer. He pays in fulfillment of the mandate of the local legislature. Not the state. Even now [Alabama] does not offer a suggestion that in passing the unemployment law she was affected by duress. . . . The difficulty with petitioner's contention is that it confuses motive with coercion. . . . But to hold that motive or temptation is equivalent to coercion is to plunge the law in endless difficulties. The outcome of such a doctrine is the acceptance of a philosophical determinism by which choice becomes impossible. Till now the law has been guided by a robust common sense which assumes the freedom of the will as a working hypothesis in the solution of its problems. The wisdom of the hypotheses has illustration in this case. Nothing in the case suggests the exertion of a power akin to undue influence, if we assume that such a concept can ever be applied with fitness to the relations between state and nation. Even on that assumption the location of the point at which pressure turns into compulsion and ceases to be inducement, would be a question of degree—at times, perhaps, of fact. The point had not been reached when Alabama made her choice. We cannot say that [Alabama] was acting, not of her unfettered will, but under the strain of a persuasion equivalent to undue influence, when she chose to have relief administered under the laws of her own making, by agents of her own selection, instead of under federal laws, administered by federal patronage and with all the ensuing evils, at least to many minds, of federal patronage and power. There would be a strange irony, indeed, if her choice were now to be annulled on the basis of an assumed duress in the enactment of a statute which her courts have accepted as a true expression of her will. . . .

In ruling as we do, we leave many questions, open. We do not say that a tax is valid, when imposed by act of Congress, if it is laid upon the condition that a state may escape its operation through the adoption of a statute unrelated in subject matter to activities fairly within the scope of national policy and power. No such question is before us. . . . [13]

Justice Cardozo's opinion eloquently and forcefully expressed the arguments that were to characterize in subsequent years the debates over federally mandated programs. Consequently, it will pay to look at his arguments more closely.

First, it should be noted that federal social programs in 1935, when the Social Security Act was passed, were few in number. Even the large number enacted in the early New Deal period appeared to be exceptions rather than typical of the kind of programs they were to become.[14] Undoubtedly it did appear that "states' righters" were being overly sensitive on the matter of state sovereignty by exaggerating the likelihood that the act would be only the first step toward federal preemption of state jurisdiction. Only by hindsight can we see that states' rights fears were accurate assessments of political trends and not solely paranoid reactions to federal activities.

Second, using the sociological approach to constitutional interpretation for which he was famous, Cardozo emphasized the existence of an economic crisis as justification for this departure from traditional forms of legislation. His interpretation of the general-welfare clause was so expansive that it could embrace even the most localized crisis. The emergency argument, combined with the general-welfare clause, offered the rationale for ignoring the federalist dimension of the Constitution. This interpretation has continued to the present day, as Congress (and the media) has willingly transformed every group's cry for relief into a matter of the "general welfare" requiring federal programmatic intervention.[15]

The third, and one of the most difficult, arguments to analyze is the assertion that states were not coerced into enacting their own unemployment laws. This was a disingenuous argument, since the reason for enactment was precisely because only one state—Wisconsin—had an unemployment compensation law. It was a fear that this state would attract residents of states without such laws and thus carry a disproportionate burden of the Depression that was one of the main justifications offered in support of national legislation.

Since states without unemployment compensation laws would lose complete control over the tax monies paid to the federal government, there was a strong incentive to adhere to the conditions imposed in the program. Cardozo was quite right in saying that "to hold that motive or temptation is equivalent to coercion is to plunge the law in endless difficulties." Nevertheless, it is clear that a state faced the prospect of substantial revenue loss no matter what it did. Participation in the program was really an understandable attempt to maintain some influence in it rather than to lose entirely both tax revenue and opportunity for influence.

This is the kind of situation confronting states in all grant-in-aid programs, which is why they often try to participate in all of them irrespective of the possibility that the programs require commitment of resources which states might prefer to put elsewhere (for example, into job-training programs instead of education, or vice versa). As Cardozo pointed out, it is very difficult to distinguish between inducement and coercion; his attempted resolution of this difficulty is hardly helpful, however. Whenever he finds that a state participates in a federal program, then he finds the exercise of choice—*post hoc, ergo propter hoc.*

Finally, Cardozo leaves to the future the question—remote then, pervasive now—of the constitutionality of imposing federal conditions on the states unrelated to the function of the grant. We now refer to these as the *horizontal* or *crosscutting requirements,* such as affirmative action or public participation mandates.

What one misses in Cardozo's opinion (keeping in mind it was written in the midst of the "court-packing plan" of 1937) is a concern for the principle of constitutionalism. An event—the Depression—burst apart the limits on federal governmental activity by offering an opportunity for interpreting key phrases in the Constitution in a way quite at variance with the structure of government established in the document itself. From 1937 on, interest groups concerned with various provisions of the Social Security Act concentrated their attention not on the states, but on Washington, D.C. State government's participation in the new welfare system was increasingly reduced to a mere formality. It is this type of authority cost emanating from the foundation principle of constitutionalism that has been ignored by writers on intergovernmental relations.

An attempt by the Supreme Court in *National League of Cities* v. *Usury,* 39 years later, to reinvigorate the structure of federalism arose in the context of a dispute over an amendment to the Fair Labor Standards Act (FLSA) of 1938.[16] The act itself had been upheld in 1941 in *United States* v. *Darby Lumber Co.* as a proper exercise of congressional power to regulate interstate commerce.[17] The 1974 amendment under challenge extended the minimum-wages and maximum-hours requirement to employees of the states and their political subdivisions.

Justice Rehnquist, in delivering the opinion for the Court, was faced with two precedents that appeared to justify extending the FLSA to state employees. In 1968 the Court had upheld an amendment to the act extending minimum-wage coverage to nonadministrative employees of state schools and hospitals.[18] And in 1975 the Court upheld federal wage and salary controls imposed on state employees under the Economic Stabilization Act of 1970.[19] Consequently, the further extension of FLSA to all state employees appeared logical.

In a 5 to 4 decision, however, the Court asserted that despite the breadth of congressional authority under the commerce clause, authority to extend wage and hour controls to nonfederal governments was limited by other constitutional provisions—in this case, by the Tenth Amendment:

> It is one thing to recognize the authority of Congress to enact laws regulating individual business necessarily subject to the dual sovereignty of the government of the Nation and of the State in which they reside. It is quite another to uphold a similar exercise of congressional authority directed not to private citizens, but to the States as States. We have repeatedly recognized that there are attributes of sovereignty attaching to every state government which may not be impaired by Congress not because Congress may lack an affirmative grant of legislative authority to reach the matter, but because the Constitution prohibits it from exercising the authority in that manner. . . .

> Our examination of the effect of the 1974 amendments, as sought to be extended to the States and their political subdivisions, satisfies us that both the minimum wage and the maximum hour provisions will impermissibly interfere with the integral governmental functions of these bodies. . . . We do not believe particularized assessments of actual impact are crucial to resolution of the issue presented, however. For even if we accept appellee's assessments concerning the impact of the amendments, their application will nonetheless significantly alter or displace the States' abilities to structure employer-employee relationships in such areas as fire prevention, police protection, sanitation, public health, and parks and recreation. These activities are typical of those performed by state and local governments in discharging their dual functions of administering the public law and furnishing public services. Indeed, it is functions such as these which governments are created to provide, services such as these which the States have traditionally afforded their citizens. If Congress may withdraw from the States the authority to make those fundamental employment decisions upon which their systems for performance of these functions must rest, we think there would be little left of the States' "separate and independent existence." . . . [t]his exercise of congressional authority does not comport with the federal system of government embodied in the Constitution. We hold that insofar as the challenged amendments operate to directly displace the States' freedom to structure integral operations in areas of traditional governmental functions, they are not within the authority granted Congress by Article I, 8, clause 3.[20]

Unlike Justice Cardozo, Rehnquist's concern is with ensuring the continued existence of at least a core of undiluted state authority. Being able to determine the ratio of full-time to part-time employees and to structure employer-employee relationships are essential factors in the performance of routine state functions. However, this case stands alone since the late 1930s in emphasizing the constitutional position of the states. Except for decisions requiring individuals to use state legal procedures before seeking the assistance of the federal judiciary, the constitutional record since the

National League of Cities case is devoid of further attempts to reinvigorate state sovereignty.

Fiscal Context of Intergovernmental Relations

The fiscal relationship between federal and state governments reflects, if it does not control, the legal relationship. As federal legal influence spread through the economy over the years, so did its fiscal influence over state and local governments. In 1979, public-sector spending (that is, all levels of government) totaled $764 billion, or about 33 percent of the Gross National Product (compared with $131 billion, or 27 percent, in 1959). Of this, about 11 percent of GNP was expended by state and local governments and 22 percent by the federal government. However, 11.6 percent of GNP, or about one-half of the federal budget, was returned to state and local governments in the form of aid.[21]

This 11.6 percent (about $83 billion in 1980) does not adequately reflect the real influence which the federal government exerts over state and local governments, however. The federal contribution now represents 26 percent of state and local expenditures up from 15 percent in 1965.[22] Since much of the federal contribution requires matching funds from the states in a ratio of $3 for every federal dollar, the federal government effectively controls almost a third of total state and local expenditures.

In 1979, the largest proportion of federal aid, 75 percent, was in the form of categorical grants; revenue sharing constituted a little over 10 percent of the total, and block grants constituted the remainder. With the possible exclusion of the states from revenue sharing, an even higher proportion of federal aid will be funneled through categorical grants, thus increasing federal controls and reversing the "new federalism" advanced in 1972, when revenue sharing was first enacted, of allowing the states greater discretion in setting their own priorities.

Categorical Grants. Federal monies are not distributed evenly across the 491 programs described in the Catalog of Federal Domestic Assistance. The bulk of federal assistance (81 percent) is channeled into 25 programs, leaving only 19 percent to be distributed among the remaining 466 programs. The largest amounts of money now are spent in the fields of natural resources, environment, health, income security, and education and training.[23]

In addition, the Advisory Commission on Intergovernmental Relations has estimated that almost 70 percent of categorical aid is distributed as formula-based grants. One-quarter is allotted by entitlement formulas, which generally contain indicators reflecting need of recipients. The largest number of grants, however, are project grants that require application by state or local governments. Although making up two-thirds of the total number of grants, they constitute less than one-third of the total federal grant monies. Generally, project grants are designed for use in urban areas, particularly to test new approaches to urban redevelopment.[24]

Block Grants. In an effort to reduce the administrative and compliance costs associated with categorical grants, the Nixon administration consolidated a number of those comprising a common functional area. Seventeen categorical grants were consolidated into a comprehensive employment and training program in 1973. The following year, social-service grants were consolidated into a block-grant program in Title XX of the Social Security Act. Since then, categorical grants have been consolidated in the areas of community development, health, public works, law enforcement, and school aid to federally affected areas.[25]

Block grants reached a peak of 14 percent of federal-aid funds in 1979, but were expected to decline thereafter. Further consolidation of categorical grants has not occurred because of a suspicion that block grants are not economically efficient and because interest groups at the national level do not wish to lose control over the existing grants.[26]

Revenue Sharing. General-purpose grants offer unrestricted allocations of money to states and local governments. They constituted less than 10 percent of federal fiscal aid in 1980, when state participation in the program was sharply curtailed. Their attraction has been a broad, "no-strings" distribution of federal funds that could provide a measure of flexibility to state and local authorities to meet local conditions.

For our purposes, the significance of the different types of grant programs lies in their respective susceptibilities to federal authority. Federal influence is maximized in categorical grants, is less in block grants, and is least in general revenue sharing.

The counterpart to this is that the ability of the federal government to determine and effectuate national policy varies inversely with the degree of state and local control. If one prefers national policymaking across the board, then the federal government should rely solely on categorical grants. If one wishes a national policy of maximum political decentralization, then general revenue sharing should be preferred.

One may conclude from the foregoing that federal grant-in-aid programs have been growing in their fiscal contribution to state- and local-government revenues. Even if their rate of growth should taper off in a period of national economic austerity, the funds will continue to be significant. Paul Posner and Stephen Sorett offer a perceptive comment on this situation:

The notion that a state or local government is free to accept or reject federal funds is becoming increasingly difficult to accept as the role of these disbursements swells. The argument can be made quite forcefully now that general revenue sharing together with the five block grant programs constitute significant, if not vital, funds sources for state and local governments. While it may be true that the refusal of one particular categorical grant will not cause "coercive" or "catastrophic" financial results, the cumulative effect can be devastating.[27]

This view reflects a consensus in the literature that subnational governments have become constitutionally and economically dependent on federal policy initiatives. What also needs to be pointed out, however, is that even the state's management of its internal organization has substantially eroded and that this constitutes a serious authority cost. Subsequent case studies will illustrate how these occur in regulations and in practice.

Characteristics of Regulation

As Murray L. Weidenbaum has emphasized, "Government regulation is an accepted fact in a modern society."[28] Even more, regulation by government has been a fact in every society throughout history and will remain so as long as organized society exists. However, the degree and type of regulation differ from society to society and carry with them differential distributions of costs to and benefits for society and individuals and groups within society. In addition, the expectations of individuals and groups influence the character of regulation and carry with them their own incentives and disincentives.

Expectations may relate to the degree and type of regulation as well as to whom the appropriate regulations should be directed. At both the federal and local levels in the United States in the nineteenth and early twentieth centuries, expectations of government regulatory functions were limited to the traditional police powers (which included the preservation of peace), protection against fire and epidemics, maintenance of a legal system, provision of some form of education, and maintenance of roads and of a postal service. Not until the 1880s was there a drive for regulation of new sectors of the economy and, in the early 1900s, regulation of wages, hours, and conditions of work.[29]

By the early years of the New Deal, government intervention in society for attainment of positive national goals rather than merely for protection against untoward events or criminal activity became accepted by a majority of the public. Table 1-1 provides one measure of the recent growth of federal regulation. Federal-government intervention to spur economic growth was legitimized in the Employment Act of 1946, and in the social

Table 1-1
Growth of Fifty-Seven Federal Regulatory Agencies, Selected Fiscal Years, 1971-1981
(*billions of dollars*)

	Expenditures					
Area	1971	1977	1978	1979	1980 (est.)	1981 (est.)
Social regulation consumer safety and health	$0.6	$1.8	$2.3	$2.5	$2.6	$2.9
Job safety and other working conditions	0.1	0.5	0.5	0.6	0.7	0.8
Energy and the environment	9.1	1.0	1.3	1.5	1.7	2.2
	$0.8	$3.3	$4.1	$4.6	$5.0	$5.9
Economic regulation						
Finance and banking	$0.1	$0.2	$0.3	$0.3	$0.3	$0.3
Other industry-specific	0.2	0.3	0.3	0.3	0.4	0.4
General business	0.1	0.2	0.2	0.3	0.3	0.3
	$0.4	$0.7	$0.8	$0.9	$1.0	$1.0
Total	$1.2	$4.0	$4.9	$5.5	$6.0	$6.9
Total in 1970 dollars [a]	$1.2	$2.6	$3.0	$3.0	$3.1	$3.2
Permanent Full-Time Positions (*thousands*)						
Social regulation	10.8	58.4	61.9	63.6	65.4	66.2
Economic regulation	18.3	23.6	24.3	23.9	24.5	24.6
Total	29.1	82.0	86.2	87.5	89.9	90.8

Source: Center for the Study of American Business, Washington University. Reprinted from *Regulation* (March/April 1980):8.

[a] Adjusted by GNP deflator (actual and, for 1980-81, estimated in 1981 budget).

sector, the civil rights acts of the late 1950s were designed to attain racial harmony. However, it was the 1960s and 1970s that brought the most dramatic increases in social regulation with the passage of vastly more powerful civil rights acts, health acts (for example, Cigarette Labeling and Advertising Act, Child Protection Act, Traffic Safety Act, Medicare, and Medicaid), environmental acts (for example, National Environment Policy Act, Clean Air Act Amendments, and Occupational Safety and Health Act), education acts, and pension security programs. The cumulation of these laws ordering and forbidding actions by individuals, businesses, schools, and health practitioners brought with them hundreds of regulations. Table 1-2 displays by time period the number of federal regulations

Table 1-2
Issuance of Federal Regulations, By Time Period

								Total
1941-1945	*1946-1950*	*1951-1955*	*1956-1960*	*1961-1965*	*1966-1970*	*1971-1975*	*1976-1978*	*1941-1978*
13	9	2	4	22	136	660	413	1255

Source: Adapted from, C.H. Lovell et al., *Federal and State Mandating on Local Governments* (Riverside, Calif.: Univ. of California, 1979), p. 72.

imposed on just state and local governments alone that were inventoried in a study by the University of California at Riverside.

Because of the federal nature of American government and the tradition of local accountability, implementation of many of these mandates was left to state and local governments, although required by the national government. However, national policy priorities may not be the same at the subnational as at the national level, nor may socioeconomic conditions be standard throughout the nation. For example, national policymakers might (and did) create a federal employment program to reduce national unemployment, while in fact, some sections of the country had low unemployment yet felt they must yield to the political pressures on them (that is, to get "their share" of the money or to accommodate an officious federal administrator). The result has been a shift in local priorities to accommodate federal ones. This, of course, also means a waste of money.[30]

Types of Regulation

All regulations are not the same, and the different types raise different theoretical questions. Table 1-3 lists the fundamental types.

In the private sector, the oldest type of regulation is that designed to remedy some kind of perceived abuse in an industry. For example, criticism of railroad rebates led to the establishment of the Interstate Commerce Commission, and a health threat by the tobacco industry led to enactment of Cigarette Labeling Act. Economywide mandates include antitrust provi-

Table 1-3
Type of Mandate by Sector

Private sector:	Industry-Specific	Economywide
Public sector:	Program-specific	Crosscutting

sions, occupational health and safety, and affirmative action requirements. They apply to all industries within the economy irrespective of any
danger that a specific business poses to employees or the public.

In the public sector, program-specific mandates include matching
requirements, single state agency requirements, and various kinds of reporting requirements. Public-sector crosscutting mandates include antidiscrimination, anticorruption, and public-participation requirements. Needless to
say, there is considerable overlap between the two sectors because some
laws are written to apply to both. Table 1–4 lists current crosscutting regulations.

Nevertheless, it is necessary to keep in mind the distinction between the
two, particularly when trying to identify costs. Private-sector costs are inflationary in nature, and benefits tend to be redistributive. Murray Weidenbaum has estimated inflationary costs in 1979 to be over $100 billion, not
including secondary costs (which also should be considered even if dollar
figures cannot be attached to them).[31] These costs would include reduced
productivity in the economy, reduced innovation (such as the introduction

Table 1–4
Inventory of National Policy and Administrative Requirements

Socioeconomic Policy Requirements

A. Nondiscrimination

Nonconstruction activities

1. Civil Rights Act of 1964, Title VI (race, color, or national origin).
2. Age Discrimination Act of 1975
3. Title IX of the Education Act Amendments of 1972, as amended.

   Housing

4. Title VIII of the Civil Rights Act of 1968.

   Handicapped

5. Section 504 of the Rehabilitation Act of 1973, as amended.
6. Architectural Barriers Act of 1968, as amended.

   Alcoholics

7. Comprehensive Alcohol Abuse and Alcoholism Prevention, Treatment, and
   Rehabilitation Act of 1970.

   Drug Abusers

8. Drug Abuse Office and Treatment Act of 1972, as amended.

Construction Activities

9. E.O. 11246, September 24, 1965, Part III.

Table 1-4 continued

B. Environmental Protection

    10. National Environmental Policy Act of 1969, as amended.
    11. Section 508 of the Federal Water Pollution Control Act Amendments of 1972 (Clean Water Act).
    12. Title XIV, Public Health Service Act, as amended.
    13. Conformity of Federal activities with State implementation plans under the Clean Air Act Amendments of 1977.
    14. Section 306 of Clean Air Act, as amended by the Clean Air Amendments of 1970.
    15. Endangered Species Act of 1973, as amended.
    16. Floodplain Management, Executive Order 11988, May 24, 1977.
    17. Protection of Wetlands, Executive Order 11990, May 24, 1977.
    18. National Flood Insurance Act of 1968, as amended by Flood Disaster Protection Act of 1973.
    19. Fish and Wildlife Coordination Act of 1934.
    20. Section 106 of the National Historical Preservation Act of 1966, as amended.
    21. Procedures for the Protection of Historic and Cultural Properties (36 C.F.R. 800).
    22. Executive Order 11593, May 31, 1971, Protection and Enhancement of the Cultural Environment.
    23. Wild and Scenic Rivers Act of 1968, as amended.
    24. Sections 307(c) and (d) of the Coastal Zone Management Act of 1972, as amended. Construction activities (grantee contracts)
    25. Archaeological and Historic Preservation Act.

C. Protection and Advancement of Economy

    26. Cargo Preference Act of 1954.
    27. Use of U.S. Flag air carriers, International Air Transportation Fair Competitive Practices Act of 1974.
    28. Placement of procurement and facilities in labor-surplus areas, 32A C.F.R. Part 134.

D. Health, Welfare and Safety

    29. Protection of human subjects of biomedical and behavioral research.
    30. Lead-based paint poisoning prohibition.
    31. Animal Welfare Act of 1966.

E. Minority Participation

    32. Indian self-determination and education assistance.
    33. Executive Order 12138 of May 18, 1979, Creating a National Women's Business Enterprise Policy.

F. Labor Standards

    Grantee contracts only

    34. Davis-Bacon Act.
    35. Anti-Kickback (Copeland) Act.
    36. Contract Work Hours and Safety Standards Act.

Administrative and Fiscal Policy Requirements

A. Public Employee Standards

    37. Intergovernmental Personnel Act of 1970, as amended.
    38. The Hatch Act.

Table 1–4 continued

B. Administrative and Procedural Requirements

   39. Federal Grant and Cooperative Agreement Act of 1977.
   40. OMB Circular No. A–40: *Management of Federal Reporting Requirements.*
   41. OMB Circular No. A–95. *Evaluation, Review, and Coordination of Federal and Federally-Assisted Programs and Projects,* revised January 13, 1976.
   42. OMB Circular No. A–111: *Jointly Funded Assistance to State and Local Governments and Nonprofit Organizations—Policies and Procedures, July 6, 1976.*
   43. Executive Order 12044: *Improving Government Regulations,* March 23, 1978.
   44. *Department of Commerce Directives for the Conduct of Federal Statistical Activities,* May 1978 (Formerly OMB Circular No. A–46).
   45. FMC 74–8: *Guidelines for Agency Implementation of the Uniform Relocation Assistance and Real Property Acquisition Policies of 1970 Public Law 91–646,* October 4, 1976.
   46. Treasury Circular No. 1082: *Notification to States of Grant-in-Aid Information,* August 8, 1973.
   47. Treasury Circular No. 1075 (Fourth Revision): *Regulation Governing the Withdrawal of Cash From Treasury for Advance Payments under Federal Grant and Other Programs,* December 14, 1947.
   48. Claims Collection Act of 1966.

C. Recipient-Related Administrative and Fiscal Requirements

   Nonprofit organizations and institutions

   49. OMB Circular No. A–21 (Formerly FMC 73–8, December 19, 1973): *Cost Principles for Education Institutions,* March 6, 1979.
   50. OMB Circular No. A–110: *Grants and Agreements with Institutions of Higher Education, Hospitals and Other Nonprofit Organizations—Uniform Administrative Requirements,* July 30, 1976.
   51. FMC 73–3: *Cost Sharing on Federal Research,* December 4, 1976.
   52. OMB Circular No. A–88 (Formerly FMC 73–6): *Coordinating Indirect Cost Rates and Audit at Educational Institutions,* December 5, 1979.
   53. FMC 73–7: *Administration of College and University Research Grants,* December 19, 1973.

   State and/or local governments

   54. OMB Circular No. A–90: *Cooperating with State and Local Governments to Coordinate and Improve Information Systems,* September 21, 1968.
   55. OMB Circular No. A–102: *Uniform Administrative Requirements for Grants-in-Aid to State and Local Governments,* revised August 24, 1977.
   56. OMB Circular No. A–73 (Formerly FMC 73–2): *Audit of Federal Programs,* March 15, 1978.
   57. FMC 74–4: *Cost Principles Applicable to Grants and Contracts with State and Local Governments,* July 18, 1974.

D. Access to Information

   58. Freedom of Information Act.
   59. Privacy Act of 1974.
   60. Family Educational Rights and Privacy Act of 1974.

Source: Adapted from *Managing Federal Assistance in the 1980's,* Office of the Management and Budget, 1980.

of new drugs), reduced purchasing power of low-income people because of federally induced price increases, and federally induced manpower shortages (such as for industrial hygienists to make OSHA-mandated inspections). This is, emphatically, not to say that there are no benefits. Cleaner air and water, reduced energy consumption, and increased job safety and health are valuable in themselves. The difficulty is in finding the least-cost method for obtaining a cluster of benefits, and many students of government regulation have suggested that there are less costly ways of attaining an acceptable cluster than the way it was being done between 1965 and 1980.

In the public sector, the kinds and relative importance of regulatory costs are different. Indeed traditional fiscal costs can be identified. For example, the state of Virginia found that it cost over $350,000 per year for it to administer the federally mandated A-95 process.[32] However, since the A-95 process is a purely communication and coordination mechanism, there is little observable behavior and no tangible product that can be quantified for purposes of estimating benefits. In such situations, one must rely on the testimony of state officials that, on the whole, it is or is not worthwhile.

In an innovative study designed to obtain concrete figures on the incremental costs to seven municipalities of complying with the Clean Water Act, Aid to the Handicapped, Bilingual Education Act, and Unemployment Compensation Act, Thomas Muller and Michael Fix found per capita costs ranging from $6 to $51 with an average cost of $24. In 1978, "the incremental cost of mandates, on the average, equalled the total revenue sharing funds received by the seven jurisdictions. . . ." They also found that state operating and capital outlays, excluding administrative costs, raised the per capita average increases to $28.[33]

While fiscal cost estimates are important for reemphasizing the fact that federal mandates are not cost free and indeed can impose substantial operating and maintenance costs after federal contributions cease (as in the case of state maintenance of highways built with a 90 percent federal contribution), they do not address the preliminary questions of (1) whether there should be such programs and (2) whether there are authority costs to the system in the participation of states in federally mandated programs. The following section inquires into the nature of the second question. To answer the first would require a detailed analysis of each individual program, a task beyond our resources at the present time.

Selected Federal Mandates

For our purposes, we shall consider a *mandate* to be a federal legislative or executive effort to condition the behavior of state or local agencies. A legislative effort may be found in a congressional statute, in an "understanding" alluded to in a congressional committee report, in an executive order, in rules issued by an administrative agency, or in a condition inserted in an intergovernmental grant. Although increasingly important, orders issued by a federal court are not included here. It also should be recalled that a mandate may be unrelated to the specific purpose of a grant, as is usually the case with crosscutting requirements.

State officials have not been averse to pointing out deficiencies in intergovernmental programs. Their complaints range from a dislike of an entire program to a small detail in a relatively unknown one. Their more politically significant complaints, however, can be categorized as follows:

1. Federal preemption of state programs unless the state meets the conditions specified in the federal mandate (for example, the Mining Safety Act).
2. Required standardization of *state* rules, which runs counter to the diverse conditions which may have justified the use of grants-in-aid in the first place (for example, federal wetlands legislation).
3. Federal use of grants to bypass the state and go directly to local governments (for example, welfare and highway programs).
4. The attachment of conditions that significantly delay or complicate implementation (for example, antidiscrimination or citizen-participation provisions).

These categories all bear on authority costs to the states which they cannot avoid. In addition to these substantive criticisms are technical administrative complaints that could be resolved through improved communication between governments. Table 1-5 lists some of these.

In a recent study of one small town, the United States Regulatory Council found the following perceptions of regulatory programs, both federal and state:[34]

1. Citizens see little or no relation between regulation of their activities and the social objectives of the regulations.
2. Lawyers, accountants, and bureaucrats are seen as the primary beneficiaries of government regulation.
3. Administrators, whether federal or state, are seen as too rigid in their dealings at the local level.
4. Federal regulation saddles some communities with the burden of responding to problems that are caused or are occurring elsewhere.

What is one to make of the preceding items? First, it should be noted that the first four categories of complaints address substantive issues that imply the need for significant changes in the intergovernmental grant struc-

Table 1-5
Federal Grant-in-Aid Programs—Major Administrative Complaints by the States

---

1. Incompatible application processes, timetables, and needs assessments (for example, education programs).
2. Different interpretations of a statute among federal agencies (for example, the Uniform Relocation and Real Property Acquisition Policy Act).
3. Lack of fungibility authority.
4. Disagreement among federal agencies on how to measure environmental impacts (for example, between EPA and FAA).
5. Federal agencies use advisory responsibilities to leverage themselves into decision-making positions (for example, Land and Water Conservation Act administered by the Department of Interior).
6. Excessive paperwork requirements (for example, Federal Highway Administration and EEOC requirements).
7. Frequently changing federal regulations (for example, federal air-pollution requirements).
8. Constant updating of "state plan" requirements (for example, Federal Water Pollution Act).
9. Frequent demand from federal agencies for special reports on a quick turnaround basis (for example, Federal Highway Administration requests for lists of minority businesses).
10. Federal procrastination in approving funding (for example, Urban Mass Transit Administration).

Source: Adapted from *Federal Roadblocks to Efficient State Government,* vol. 1 (Washington: National Governor's Conference, 1977).

ture. Second, the list of state administrative complaints can be met by improved coordination techniques, many of which already are in place. Third, the complaints and criticisms from citizens and state and local officials alike suggest a long and deep-seated resentment of federal regulations and regulators (whether deserved or not) and resentment over regulation in general. The remainder of this chapter analyzes particular programs to identify the means by which the federal government transforms and centralizes the allocation of authority in a policy area that results in the dilution of authority and confusion in the minds of citizens.

Crosscutting Requirements

A brief description of the administrative cumbersomeness of Equal Employment Opportunity (EEO) rules can serve as a convenient introduction to more detailed study of crosscutting requirements. State and local governments must abide by the requirements of several civil rights acts forbidding discrimination because of race, color, national origin, age, sex, or handicapped status. Any single program may be within the jurisdiction of six statutes that may have as many as seventeen or as few as seven federal agencies enforcing them (see table 1-6). State and local governments may have to report to several agencies when administering a single grant program. To illustrate further the complexity of EEO administration, there are eighty-two statutes and rules, administered by thirty-two federal agencies, governing the subject. The requirements encompass such matters as definitions of employment discrimination, compliance and enforcement, utilization of sanctions, investigations, training, data and record-keeping, publications, work sharing, memoranda of understanding, standards and job qualifications, and staff and resource needs. In addition, each state and each local political unit employing more than fifteen employees must submit an elaborate annual report to a joint EEO Commission–state agency.

A large number of grant-in-aid programs are subject to federal nonprogrammatic conditions of the type exemplified in EEO rules. Table 1-4 listed the most common ones, most of which seek objectives unrelated to the purpose of the grant itself. The assumption is that they establish national objectives that would be ignored if left to other institutions. By attaching them to grant programs offered to states or industries, it was assumed that both the localized self-interest and the national interest could be attained at minimal cost.

Yet, as a study by the Advisory Commission on Intergovernmental Relations (ACIR) pointed out, there are four frequently ignored problems associated with them: "(1) the lack of federal awareness of the costs that national policy conditions impose on grantees; (2) the inadequacy of present federal grant allocations and other funds to meet both the basic objectives of grants-in-aid and the additional goals established by national policy conditions . . . ; (3) the insensitivity of national policy conditions to the diverse needs, resources, and capacities of the state and local government grantees; and (4) the ineffective interagency coordination of national policy conditions and the consequent inconsistencies among agency regulations issued pursuant to each condition."[35]

Environmental Protection. Among the most complex federal regulations are those relating to environmental protection. The fundamental statute is the National Environmental Policy Act of 1969 (NEPA), which requires that all proposed federal plans, programs, regulations, and financial-assistance programs must be reviewed to determine whether they have a "significant" impact on the environment. (However, NEPA does not apply to state participation in general revenue-sharing.) If such impact is found, a detailed environmental-impact statement (EIS) is required. While all agencies must conduct such impact studies, it is the responsibility of the Council on Environmental Quality to coordinate them.

NEPA may apply even before a state has requested federal aid, if the state project has received federal location approval. Although not strictly a regulatory program, the EIS requirement attaches to a wide variety of

Table 1–6
Number of Federal Agencies Enforcing Civil Rights Statutes

Federal Statute	Number of Enforcing Agencies
Civil Rights Act of 1964	17
Section 504	15
Age Discrimination	7
Title IX	7

Source: EEOC Survey Responses, 1980.

grant-in-aid programs and imposes substantial fiscal costs and paperwork burdens, many of which are clearly unnecessary. ACIR noted that between 1970 and 1975, nearly 7,000 EISs were filed "costing several hundred million dollars per year."[36] Merely to process the EISs in the federal aid-to-highways program cost almost $5 million and fifteen man-months.[37]

The purpose of EISs leaves considerable room for individual interpretation. The regulations state than an EIS "is to serve as an action-forcing device to insure that the policies and goals defined in the Act are infused into the ongoing programs and actions of the Federal Government." This masterpiece of bureaucratic clarity is not made more precise by subsequent elaborations. However, among the requirements are the inclusion of discussions of "direct effects and their significance" and "indirect effects and their significance," the environmental effects of alternatives, and the assessment of not only the physical effects, but also those dealing with "urban quality" and social impacts (matters on which there is no scientific consensus).[38]

One of the consequences is the use of these amorphous requirements as bases for private groups to bring law suits in order to delay projects to which they are opposed. Between 1970 and 1975, over 650 such law suits were initiated. After its examination of NEPA, ACIR also found one of its consequences to be for grantees "to shop around for grants from agencies with the 'easiest' environmental review requirements." Consequently, many states, seventeen, in fact, have decided not to develop any environmental-impact statements at all, leaving such requirements to the national government.[39]

Even without duplication of requirements, however, most grantees must consider whether an impact statement is required of them. Meeting the impact-statement requirements incurs costs, causes program delays, and tends to shift the focus of attention from the substantive goals of the grant to the impact-statement process. The split authority over environmental programs further generates a certain level of cynicism among the various government actors, as the Council of State Governments has observed:

Environmental programs exacerbate the continuing tension between state and local governments over the distribution of authority and program administration. Regulations for air and water quality may be imposed by federal agencies, but local governments often view state agencies as the culprit. In some states, agencies are hesitant to rely on local governments to implement environmental programs. In some instances, local officials who fail to comply with environmental standards or to administer delegated responsibilities are perceived as part of the problem in enforcing environmental programs. [40]

Rights of the Handicapped. In 1973, enactment of section 504 of the Rehabilitation Act prohibited discrimination against or denial of benefits to otherwise qualified handicapped individuals by any federally funded program inclusive of all grants-in-aid. Each federal agency was required to develop and promulgate regulations to carry out the purposes of the act.

The 1973 act was subsequently expanded in 1975 in the Education for All Handicapped Children Act and in 1978 by the Rehabilitation, Comprehensive Services, and Developmental Disabilities Act. In the meantime, Executive Order 11914 gave responsibility to the Department of Health, Education and Welfare (HEW) to coordinate regulations by various federal agencies.

The overriding goal of the original legislation, as enunciated by Senator Dole, was "to assist handicapped individuals in achieving their full potential for participation in our society." Determining who the handicapped are and the type of accommodations to be made for them is left to agency regulation and court definition. The regulations issued by HEW and the Department of Transportation (DOT) illustrate the complexity of the problem. [41]

Embraced by the acts are not only direct but also indirect recipients of federal financial assistance and any of their successors to such assistance. Appendix A to the regulations lists 154 federal and 32 state-administered programs affected. The latter include library, vocational education, community service, old-age assistance, and community health programs.

Among the regulations to which states and other recipients must adhere are

1. Prohibition of the use of criteria that have the purpose or effect (!) of defeating or substantially impairing accomplishment of the objectives of the recipient's program with respect to handicapped persons or that perpetuate the discrimination of another recipient if both recipients are subject to common administrative control or are agencies of the same state.
2. In determining the site of facility, a recipient may not make selections that have the effect of excluding handicapped persons.

3. An assurance of compliance with the regulations obligates the recipient for the entire period of assistance to ensure that the buildings are used for the purpose for which federal assistance was once extended.
4. Where a recipient is found to have discriminated against a person in violation of section 504 and where another recipient exercises control over the recipient that has discriminated, the Director of the Office of Civil Rights (HEW) may require either or both recipients to take remedial action.
5. The director may order a recipient to take remedial action with respect to handicapped persons who are no longer in a program or would have been in a program if the discrimination had not occurred.
6. In cooperation with handicapped persons or their organizations, a recipient must evaluate the agency's current policies and programs as they relate to section 504 regulations.
7. A recipient employing more than fifteen persons must designate at least one person to coordinate its efforts to comply with section 504.
8. Section 504 regulations supersede state and local laws that prohibit or limit the eligibility of qualified handicapped persons to receive services or to practice any occupation.
9. A recipient must design its programs to make them readily accessible to handicapped persons. This may include redesign of equipment and reassignment of services to accessible buildings.
10. Buildings used by the recipient must be altered or new ones designed to make them readily accessible to handicapped persons.

Dozens of other regulations have been issued by HEW affecting states along with other federal recipients. No special funds have been made available for complying with section 504, although grant monies may be used for that purpose. One may reasonably assume that grant applications have been inflated to meet these increased costs, thus effectively reducing the money available for the primary purpose of the grant. In 1979, HEW-sponsored studies estimated that one-time structural modification costs required by the regulations would range from $1.2 to $5.7 billion (depending on whether one uses HEW estimates or recipients' estimates). Postsecondary education costs average $53 per student; recurring costs (for example, interpreter costs for deaf students, busing handicapped students) were estimated to be $50 million per year; maintenance costs (for example, for elevators), $50 million per year; and $20 to $50 million per year for new construction costs (though this is less than 1 percent of total new construction costs of HEW recipients).[42]

The regulations implementing section 504 in the Department of Transportation also have raised considerable controversy in both the public and private sectors. Under the regulations, transit systems must equip buses with lifts for wheelchairs, install elevators in undergound and aboveground rail stations, and modify rail cars to accommodate wheelchairs. A study by the Congressional Budget Office in 1979 estimated that the cost of making additions or alterations to buses and subways would amount to $400,000 for each new wheelchair user. Each trip by a wheelchair user would cost about $37.[43]

Overlooked or ignored by the federal regulations are the variety of conditions throughout the country that impose disproportionate costs on state and local governments. For example, cities that have a number of hills are not conducive to people in wheelchairs, and in northern cities, the weather makes it impossible for wheelchair users to approach or to wait at bus stops. Another condition is the varied abilities of local governments to meet the costs of the regulations. Cleveland estimated that it would need $53 million and Philadelphia $650 million to retrofit its transit system to meet DOT's requirements. Both cities are already in the throes of fiscal crisis.

Trying to accommodate the needs of the handicapped is another example of a laudatory goal that imposes costs on state and local governments out of all proportion to the benefits. Not only must they bear the brunt of the economic costs, but their pursuit of objectives which they find to be immediately pressing is diluted by the need to meet numerous complex federal regulations unrelated to local priorities. States have had to reorganize their administrative systems, as state governors have had to establish liaison offices to work with various agencies and with the state legislatures in order to change state laws at odds with the federal requirements. Appropriations also have had to be enacted to ensure state compliance with section 504.[44]

Occupational Safety and Health. The Occupational Safety and Health Act (OSHA) of 1970 was enacted "to assure safe and healthful working conditions for working men and women." A subordinate unit within the Department of Labor, the Occupational Safety and Health Administration, has the responsibility to establish and enforce safety and health standards for all organizations engaged in interstate commerce. OSHA is but one of seventy-five health-related grant-in-aid programs, but it is surely the most far-reaching in its preemption of one of the most well-established police powers of state governments.

As it began to enforce regulations on private businesses, OSHA immediately became a subject of controversy, despite the fact that it had passed both houses of Congress by overwhelming majorities. By 1972, concerted efforts were begun to modify the original act. Amendments were added in 1974, 1976, 1977, and 1979, each designed to exempt from coverage certain categories of business (based on number of employees) or to reduce inspections.

Critics of OSHA argued that injuries in many industries were negligible and that safety standards issued by OSHA were frequently unrealistic. In addition, a number of studies appeared which emphasized the apparent contribution of OSHA regulations to inflationary pressures in the economy. For example, OSHA-imposed incremental costs of forty-eight large companies were estimated by Arthur Anderson and Co. to be $184 million in 1977.[45]

In 1978, however, attention began to be given to the role of the states in the program. The act offered the opportunity for them to assume responsibility for the program. If they did, they had to submit a state plan for the development of standards and means of enforcement. Such a plan could lead to state assumption of full responsibility for the program, subject to federal monitoring, or to a shared administration and inspection with the federal government. A third alternative, of course, was to decline the invitation and thus leave full responsibility with the federal government.

If the state did participate, the federal government funded 50 percent of its costs. Somewhat surprisingly, OSHA provides 90 percent funding to states and private consultants for on-site consultation, an alternative to comprehensive administration. This has served as an incentive for some states to forego complete participation in favor of special consultation agreements. In 1980, for example, only eight states had approved comprehensive plans, but another thirteen had opted for the consultation agreements (which avoided enforcement inspections). Five states had withdrawn their plans before being approved, and another seven withdrew after the plans were approved. Only twenty-one states, consequently, were participating in the grant program, and one of these, Virginia, which had an approved plan, was suing OSHA over allegedly arbitrary enforcement procedures. From this survey, it is clearly an understatement to say that states have been less than happy with OSHA legislation and administration.

One need go no further than the act and its implementing regulations to discern reasons for this general lack of enthusiasm. The act begins innocuously enough by stating that the federal government will not preempt state standards relating to health and welfare, *providing* the state adheres to certain requirements. It is worth listing these to gain an appreciation for their cumulative impact on a state administrative system:

1. Continuance of state enforcement requires maintenance of current state effort without diminution in the level of state enforcement activity. This is conditional upon submission and approval by OSHA of a state plan.

2. The governor is required to designate a single state agency to enter into an agreement with OSHA.
3. OSHA has the discretion to determine the degree of specificity of state standards.
4. The number of state reports is determined solely by OSHA.
5. Plans that "unduly" burden interstate commerce will not be approved.
6. State standards must be at least as "effective" as the federal standards.
7. The state plan must prohibit advance notice of inspections of business sites.
8. State personnel must be employed on a merit basis, and such system must be approved by the U.S. Office of Personnel Management.
9. The state must devote "adequate" funds to the administration and enforcement of the program.
10. The state plan must, to the extent permitted by state law, include all state and local employees in the program.
11. States must require of employers the same records and reports to be submitted to OSHA "as if the plan were not in effect."
12. States must develop indices of effectiveness and provide factual information showing its plan is as effective as OSHA's.
13. States must provide opportunity for public participation in the development of standards.
14. State agencies must have the requisite legal authority for enforcing standards.
15. States must provide employee appeals procedures.
16. States must offer training and consultation opportunities to employers and employees.
17. State plans must be continuously monitored by OSHA.
18. Regional OSHA directors must evaluate state programs semiannually.
19. Any proposed changes in a state's program must be submitted to OSHA for its approval.
20. At any time, and at his own discretion, the Assistant Secretary of Labor for OSHA may reconsider his approval of a state plan.

A perusal of the twenty conditions shows that only numbers 6 and 12 could be considered substantive in nature; that is, they contribute directly to the attainment of the objectives stated in the act. The remaining conditions are procedural and relate to the oversight of state programs by OSHA. The "carrot" of 50 percent funding by OSHA is sufficient to attract participation by some states, but clearly not a substantial number. The experiences of two states illustrate some of the difficulties that have arisen.

South Carolina offers a particularly good example of what a state obligates itself to do when entering into an agreement with OSHA. It had to shift responsibility for administering health and safety coverage of agricultural employees from the state department of agriculture to the Department of Labor. The state's merit system had to be extended to include its department of labor and all state health personnel. In addition, most of its regulations for enforcement and review of contested cases had to be changed to bring them into conformity with OSHA requirements. Many of these changes required state legislation before they could go into effect.

The second example involves a lawsuit by Virginia in 1980 that emerged from a long-standing disagreement with OSHA over what constituted proper state enforcement mechanisms and appeals procedures. The Virginia plan, which had been approved by OSHA, provided for enforcement through the judicial process instead of through an administrative adjudicatory process followed by court review, as desired by OSHA. The state legislature, in 1979, had enacted legislation meeting some of the objections raised by OSHA, including the creation of a new reporting system and a new warrant system for administrative searches. However, OSHA continued to find this objectionable, and the controversy eventually reached the point where OSHA threatened to withdraw approval of the state plan and, with it, grant funds totaling $1,162,063.

What have been the political impacts on state government participation in OSHA? The state legislature, the preeminent symbol of representative government, has had to enact legislation to bring its laws into conformity with the regulations of a federal agency, even though the latter were judged by many to be inferior to some of the states. Similarly, state governors have had to reorganize their departments to bring them into conformity with OSHA regulations. In addition, states have had to adhere to particularly rigid reporting and evaluation requirements. As one state official (sympathetic to OSHA) remarked, "The imposition of monitoring, reporting and varied interpretations of directives, standards, [and so forth] took the program from the field where it belongs into the confines of offices, file cabinets and conferences."[46]

Finally, any changes in a state program must be approved by an administrator in OSHA, leaving to him the decision as to whether a state is devoting "adequate" funds to administration of the program. This undermines the state's responsibility to its citizens to reflect state priorities in its budget. When OSHA requires that a state add personnel for health inspections or to meet reporting requirements, it means that other state functions must suffer. These opportunity costs are very difficult to quantify, but they are no less real. Eventually, of course, the added costs are transferred to the private sector, but in such an indirect manner that the taxpayer seldom is aware of them.

OSHA is almost sui generis in the degree to which it preempts state authority. Except for the Voting Rights Act of 1965, as amended, there is probably no other federal program that so clearly contravenes the spirit of federalism. Yet both acts are difficult to criticize because their purposes are so obviously praiseworthy. Nevertheless, the political and constitutional costs are high indeed.

Program-Specific Mandates

Mandates associated with specific grant-in-aid programs differ considerably. However, certain requirements, such as those specifying forms of program coordination and implementation, appear with considerable frequency. A typical requirement is that a single state agency be designated, usually by the governor, as the state applicant or coordinating body. Of twenty-four programs in the health area, for instance, eleven had this as a requirement. Twenty-three of them required either a formal plan or an evaluation report to be made by the recipient, and all required recipients to ensure maintenance of state efforts at the time the grant was applied for and to submit periodic reports on their activities. The two programs described in the next two subsections illustrate the specificity of federal controls associated with what has been referred to as "cooperative federalism."

Weatherization Assistance for Low-Income Persons. Enacted as part of the National Energy Conservation Policy Act, this categorical program illustrates the complex administrative requirements involved. The program is designed to operate via grants to state and local government agencies whose applications have been accepted by the regional administrator of the Department of Energy (DOE).

To be eligible, a state had to submit a plan within 90 days of the publication of rules by DOE. The state plan must have been preceded by one or more public hearings on a proposed plan. Subsequent to the hearing, the state plan had to describe some twenty-five factors, such as the type of weatherization work to be done, mechanisms for providing sources of labor, estimates of the number of eligible dwelling units in which the elderly and the handicapped reside and the extent to which they have priority, the amount of nonfederal resources committed to the program, and assurance that funds will be allocated to a community action agency unless the governor of the state determines that the agency is ineffective. However, a local applicant may request that the state plan's allocation not be applied and that DOE's regional representative determine the allocation and priority of funds.

Other rules require each grantee to ensure that federal funds will not supplant state or local funds and "to the maximum extent practicable as determined by DOE, to increase the amounts of these funds that would be made available in the absence of Federal funds provided. . . ." The grantee, to the maximum extent practicable, must secure volunteers and train participants, and CETA public service workers must be given qualified supervision. Each state must establish a policy advisory council, and if a state does not participate in the program, the regional representative of DOE must establish one. The members of the council must be "sensitive" to the problems of low-income people and must be representative of groups representing the elderly, handicapped, and low-income Native Americans.

Additionally, regulations specify what the allowable expenditures and standards for weatherization shall be. DOE must monitor and evaluate implementation, and each grantee must keep any records that DOE might require, including quarterly performance and financial reports.

Altogether, program regulations consume eleven double-column pages in the Code of Federal Regulations, most of which contain specific rules and refer to other documents containing additional regulations. Undoubtedly, if DOE rigorously enforced these regulations, administration costs for the program could nearly equal the actual weatherization costs. In fact, the Connecticut plan for FY 1977 identified a federal allocation of $343,000 and state support costs of $515,331 for a total program cost of $858,885 to weatherize 1,619 units (that is, $530 per unit). Support costs included on-site supervisory expenses, transportation, tools, and equipment. Aside from a suspicion that $530 per unit seems rather high especially since volunteer labor is not included, the authority costs are quite evident.

The sums of money involved are not negligible, so it is understandable why states would wish to participate in the program if they could do so. The alternative would include a situation in which the state was locked out of the process as interest groups concentrated their attention and political support on local agencies and on DOE. One also can see in the regulations that the states do not have significant discretion should the DOE field representative decide to intervene firmly. The maintenance of effort stipulation, the need to consult frequently with an advisory council, and the continuous monitoring by DOE are authority costs not only to the state but to the federal government as well. When the program goes awry, as this one has in several states, one government may receive the blame for mistakes made by the other. A poorly organized effort by Connecticut, on which a congressional hearing was held, resulted in the respective state and federal officials accusing each other of maladministration.[47] In letters to DOE regional offices, Alaska, Washington, and North Dakota resoundingly criticized the agency for causing the difficulties in their respective state programs.[48]

However, it is not at all clear that both federal and state governments receive political benefits from the program owing to the efforts of just one of them. Interest groups, often the most knowledgeable about the substance of the programs, are likely to bestow their rewards on the (federal) initiators of the program, not on the actual administrators. If this is an accurate appraisal, then the states are close to a no-win situation when it comes to evaluating the success or failure of a program. The only clear advantage to the state is the additional money to run a program which they might or might not have embarked upon on their own initiative.

The Surface Mining Control and Reclamation Act (SMCR). The purpose of this act is to develop standards by which coal can be extracted and thus assist the nation in meeting its energy requirements. To do this, the act offers incentives to the states to develop regulatory programs following federal guidelines. A variety of grant-in-aid programs are authorized in the act, including one for research institutes at state colleges and another establishing a state reclamation fund that may be operated by either the Department of Interior, the Department of Agriculture, or by the state. Each state wishing to assume jurisdiction over coal surface mining is required to submit a state plan to the Department of Interior for approval. In lieu of a state plan, the Department of Interior will regulate the mining operations. Some of the federal requirements for approval of a state plan are

1. Enactment of state laws to bring the state into legal conformity with federal regulations.
2. Designation by the governor of a single state agency as the regulatory body.
3. Federal approval of the organization of the state agency.
4. Sixteen specific regulations governing the state administrative system for reviewing applications for permits to engage in surface mining, assessing fees, holding public hearings, providing judicial review, and so forth.
5. Eight specific regulations governing state submission of statistical data.
6. A description of state employees' experience, training, and job function.
7. Description of the capital and operating budget for prior, current, and the two successive fiscal years.
8. Public notice of the state plan is required to be made by the regional director of the Department of Interior (DOI).
9. DOI must receive the approval of the state plan from the Environmental Protection Agency (EPA).
10. State employees must have no indirect or direct financial interests in coal-mining operations.
11. DOI may evaluate state maintenance of its program at any time.
12. DOI may substitute federal enforcement for all or part of the state program after public notice has been given to the state.
13. Federal regulations explicitly supersede any state statutes or regulations contrary to the former.

14. The federal law authorizes any person to bring suit against either the
    federal or state government and the plaintiff may be reimbursed litiga-
    tion costs including attorney fees.

In addition to these general requirements of the grant, the Code of
Federal Regulations contains another 350 pages specifying in detail the
standards to be applied to the entire surface-mining operation. Although
the ensuing bargaining process between federal and state officials has
resulted in a relaxation of federal standards, any alterations still must have
the approval of the staff of the Office of Surface Mining (OSM) irrespective
of the wishes of the state.[49]

OSM can exercise its authority through both the grants and the inspection processes. In a study of the relationships between OSM and the designated state agency for West Virginia, the Department of Natural Resources
(DNR), the investigator found quite amicable and cooperative relations at
first because early indications were that the DNR was in accord with federal
regulations. Within a short time, however, DNR found this was not the case
when it appeared that OSM was likely to exercise considerable influence
over a subordinate division within DNR. The latter faced the possibility of
losing a portion of its authority over its own agency. One OSM official
quoted in the study expressed the OSM attitude to be "blatantly coercive
about state use of grants."[50] Moreover, Governor Rockefeller of West
Virginia testified: "Section 101(f) of the Act stands as a mandate of the
Congress which recognized the important role of the individual states.
OSM, however, by and through the rulemaking process, has failed to adhere
to that mandate. . . . OSM has consistently failed to benefit from the expertise existing in the states."[51]

It is clear that grant programs such as SMCR transform the state
agency into an arm of the federal government. The agency's responsibilities
and even structure are significantly subordinated to OSM. Neither the
governor nor the state legislature (nor, for all intents and purposes, voters
in the state) can affect the substance of the policies administered by the state
agency. A clearer example of an authority cost would be hard to find.

Conclusion

The principle of federalism is one of the three principles underlying American constitutionalism. With the separation of powers doctrine and the protection of individual rights, federalism was considered a bulwark against a
potentially authoritarian national regime. It was one more expression of the
political theory of the Framers to fragment power by using the self-interest
of one institution to check the interest (power) of another. The United

States was not understood to be unitary and indivisible except when perforing the minimally necessary functions of national defense and maintenance of internal communications. The Framers undeniably hoped the new government would work toward a stronger sense of national identity, but at the same time there is no evidence that they wished the states to disappear. More than anything else, they desired a balanced government.

Demographic, technological, and international changes led the way toward a dominant national government by the middle of the twentieth century. The preeminent political ideology of the period was characterized by optimism that an interventionist economic theory could stabilize fluctuations of the business cycle and that recently acknowledged forms of individual rights required immediate national standardization. It was felt that the diversity of the nation had been grossly exaggerated by reactionaries and beneficiaries of the status quo. In sum, any assertion of a "national interest" automatically justified federal control. If the federal government did not have legal authority to impose national policy, it could simply attain it via a grant-in-aid mechanism.

The cumulation of national policies, whether of an indirect crosscutting nature or outright supersession of state regulatory activity, has had two effects, one pragmatic and the other political. Pragmatically, the result of this trend has been to blur the distinction between a universal quality (for example, environmental quality or clean air and clean water) and differential expressions of it at the local level. Not all freshwater lakes are alike, not all irrigation projects are the same, not all coal mines constitute similar safety hazards, not all surface mining has the same impact on prime grazing lands or wildlife. What all too frequently happens is that Congress enacts legislation that asserts federal authority over particular subject matter and then leaves it to the agency to implement the details. The agency responds by issuing its standards, which are narrower than those in the legislation, but still not narrow enough to respond to the many nuances of a local situation. The process becomes even more complex because the federal middle-managers and lower-level employees charged with overseeing the program occasionally know very little about the subject matter. Thus one encounters situations, such as those that plagued OSHA and EEOC in their early years, in which the regulations did not reflect the actual dynamics of the work activity. Or the federal agency does what the Office of Surface Mining did, that is, recruit knowledgeable state officials and inspectors as their own employees. In either case, the states (and businesses) lose credibility with the public.

Concomitant with this lack of expertise is the increase in interagency coordination problems both in the federal and state governments and at the intergovernmental level. Not only does the state agency have to enter into undertakings with other state agencies, but it also must await comment or approval from several federal agencies. OSM, for example, must forward state plans to EPA for approval, plus circulate plans and any amendments. The same plans and amendments also must be reviewed by the Fish and Wildlife Service, the Department of Agriculture, the Army Corp of Engineers, the Advisory Council on Historic Preservation, and the General Accounting Office. Meeting these crosscutting requirements can lead to frustrating delays and increased confusion at the state level. A frequent result is that the states then attempt to bring political pressure on the federal agency through their congressional delegations, and this only tends to antagonize the federal agencies or to distort their internal priorities.

The shift in decision making from the local to the national level can be observed not only in the recent spate of laws and regulations, but also in the rapid increase in state, local, and private lobbying organizations in Washington. This is not only where national policy is set, it is also where local policy and priorities are determined. As groups and even local community agencies that receive federal funds shift their attention to federal agencies, so do private citizens. State government authority becomes diluted and peripheral to the interests of its citizens. This is an authority cost because the expectation of citizens is that federalism is a constitutional principle until abolished, not by congressional or court decision, but by constitutional amendment (as indeed it has been so modified in the past).

Since the federal government is not suddenly going to reverse its actions of the last 50 years, it is imperative for students of regulation to offer pragmatic suggestions for alleviating the problems rather than seeking utopian solutions. Two alternatives that could provide this alleviation are as follows:

1. Increased reliance on performance standards. Since congressional legislation is quite likely to continue to be written in sweeping terms, there should be a concurrent resolution passed expressing the sense of Congress that agencies rewrite their regulations to reflect performance criteria for evaluating state programs. While this will not solve the problem of state authority, since the standards themselves will remain controversial, it would result in a reduction of reports to federal agencies and in the need for state and local officials to solicit frequent clearances from federal officials. One must be careful, however, that what an agency calls a performance standard is not a euphemism for specific procedural conditions.

2. State legislatures should enact laws prohibiting a state official from entering into a grant-in-aid program that requires designation of a single state agency, prescribes the qualifications of state employees, or prescribes advisory or oversight commissions having particular ideological biases (for example, "sensitivity" toward particular groups in society or toward particular policy objectives). Commissions should be selected primarily for

their objective expertise relevant to the purpose of the grant and not on the basis of social attitudes.[52]

Currently, much of the congressional legislation attempting to rationalize the grant-in-aid or regulatory process is concerned with "streamlining" or improving coordination and/or providing for a legislative veto of agency rules. Neither of these will reduce the authority costs involved. Improving administration at the federal level, unless it involves surrendering some decision-making authority (and supervision) by federal agencies will simply make the subservient role of states and local governments more obvious.

An effectively enforced legislative veto will actually exacerbate authority costs because the use of it very frequently will decrease the legitimacy of all administrative decisions. If it is used sparingly, its deterrent value will be negligible, and the source of the problem will remain unaffected. The real initiative for resolving the problems raised in this chapter remains with state governments. If they do not exercise this initiative, then one may justifiably conclude that they no longer perform a useful function.

Notes

1. Milton Friedman, *Capitalism and Freedom* (Chicago: Univ. of Chicago Press, 1962); William E. Simon, *A Time for Truth* (New York: McGraw-Hill, 1978); Murray L. Weidenbaum and Robert DeFina, *The Cost of Federal Regulation of Economic Activity* (Washington: American Enterprise Institute, 1978); and Murray L. Weidenbaum, *Business, Government, and the Public* (Englewood Cliffs, N.J., Prentice-Hall, 1977).

2. The concept of cost of regulation is difficult to come to grips with. See, Weidenbaum and DeFina, *The Cost of Federal Regulation*; Congressional Budget Office, *Federal Constraints on State and Local Government Actions* (Washington: USGPO, 1979); Julius W. Allen, *Estimating the Costs of Federal Regulation* (Washington: Congressional Research Service Report No. 78-205E, 1978); the President's Advisory Council on Executive Organization, *A New Regulatory Framework* (Washington: USGPO, 1971); U.S. Domestic Council, *The Challenge of Regulatory Reform* (Washington: USGPO, 1977); General Accounting Office, *Government Regulatory Activity: Justifications, Processes, Impacts, and Alternatives* (GAO Report PAD 77-34); and Arthur Anderson and Co., *Cost of Government Regulation Study for the Business Roundtable* (New York: 1979).

3. On the general question of credibility, see James L. Sundquist, "The crisis of Competence in Government," in *Setting National Priorities Agenda for the 1980s* (Washington: Brookings Institution, 1980), pp. 531–563.

4. U.S. Advisory Commission on Intergovernmental Relations, *Categorical Grants: Their Role and Design* (Washington: USGPO, 1977); and *State Mandating of Local Expenditures* (Washington: USGPO, 1978).

5. For example, see *U.S. Senate Committee on Governmental Affairs, Regulatory Reform Legislation. Hearings, March 20, April 6 and 24, May 3, 4, 16, 18, 23, June 5, 6, 20, 1979.* 2 vols. (Washington: USGPO, 1979).

6. C.H. Lovell et al., *Federal and State Mandating on Local Governments* (Riverside, Calif.: Univ. of California, Riverside, 1979).

7. See generally, Jesse H. Choper, "The Scope of National Power Vis-à-Vis the States: The Dispensability of Judicial Review," *Yale Law Journal* 86 (July 1977):1553–1556.

8. An important point to note is that local-government entities are not referred to at all in the Constitution. This omission lends strong support to the correctness of Dillon's rule enunciated in *City of Clinton* v. *The Cedar Rapids and Missouri River Railroad* [*Iowa Law Review,* 24(1868):455]. Basically it declared that local jurisdictions are the creatures of the state and may exercise only those powers expressly granted them by the state. When one realizes that local governments, especially cities, are frequently more influential in lobbying than the states, one begins to understand the discrepancy between political reality and constitutional form.

9. For example, NLRB v. Jones and Laughlin Co., 301 U.S. 1 (1937); Wickard v. Filburn, 317 U.S. 111 (1942); Steward Machine Co. v. Davis, 301 U.S. 548 (1937); and Helvering v. Davis, 301 U.S. 619 (1937); for a discussion of the due process and equal protection clauses, see Gerald Gunther, *Cases and Materials on Constitutional Law* (Mineola, N.Y.: Foundation Press, 1975), pp. 616–689.

10. W. Brooke Graves, *American Intergovernmental Relations* (New York: Scribner's, 1964).

11. 262 U.S. 447 (1923); 301 U.S. 548 (1937).

12. Thomas J. Madden, "The Right to Receive Federal Grants and Assistance, *Federal Bar Journal* 37 (Fall 1978):17–60.

13. The logic of the *Massachusetts* v. *Mellon* and the *Steward Machine Co.* v. *Davis* cases was carried to an extreme in *United States* v. *Frazier,* 297 F.Supp. 319(M.D. Ala. 1968) when Alabama was told that once it agreed to accept grants-in-aid, it had to abide by all the conditions of the grant and could not escape them "by thereafter refusing to accept and utilize additional grant-in-aid funds." Madden "The Right to Receive Federal Grants," p. 21.

14. On the background to the Social Security Act, see Martha Derthick *Policymaking for Social Security* (Washington: Brookings Institution, 1979).

15. Daniel J. Elazar, *American Federalism: A View from the States*

(New York: Crowell, 1972), p. 34; also see E.E. Schattschneider, *The Semi-Sovereign People* (New York: Holt, Reinhart and Winston, 1975) on the theory of "socialization of conflict."

16. National League of Cities v. Usery, 426 U.S. 833 (1976).

17. 312 U.S. 100 (1941).

18. Maryland v. Wirtz, 392 U.S. 183 (1968).

19. Fry v. United States, 421 U.S. 542 (1975).

20. National League of Cities v. Usury, 426 U.S. 833 (1976).

21. OMB, "Special Analysis H," *Special Analyses: Budget of the U.S. Government: Fiscal Year 1981* (Washington: USGPO, 1980), pp. 239–257. For a summary description of the growth in federal aid and programs, see Carl W. Stenberg, "Federalism in Transition," *Intergovernmental Perspective* 6 (Winter 1980):4–13.

22. OMB "Special Analysis."

23. Ibid, p. 257.

24. Advisory Commission on Intergovernmental Relations, *Categorical Grants: Their Role and Design* (Washington: USGPO, 1978), p. 92.

25. George F. Break, "Intergovernmental Fiscal Relations," in *Setting National Priorities: Agenda for the 1980s* (Washington: Brookings Institution, 1980), pp. 256–258.

26. Ibid.

27. Paul L. Posner and Stephen M. Sorett, "A Crisis in the Fiscal Commons: The Impact of Federal Expenditures on State and Local Governments," *Public Contract Journal* 10 (December 1978): 346. ACIR also has pointed out that almost every local government in the United States received federal funds and that "federal aid found its way into three-quarters of all state agencies. . . ." ACIR, *Growth of Government* (forthcoming, 1980), p. 24.

28. *Government-Mandated Price Increases* (Washington: American Enterprise Institute, 1975), p. 3.

29. See generally, Murray L. Weidenbaum, *Business, Government, and the Public* (Englewood Cliffs, N.J.: Prentice-Hall, 1977).

30. Just such a situation is described by a local administrator. See John V. Witherspoon, "Life Among the 'Grunts'," *The Urban Interest* 2 (Spring 1980):52–58.

31. Murray L. Weidenbaum, "Measuring the Costs of Regulation," reprinted in *U.S. Senate Committee on Governmental Affairs,* pp. 1006–1007.

32. Commonwealth of Virginia, Department of Intergovernmental Affairs, "An Assessment of A-95 Effectiveness in Virginia," *Staff Report* (March 1980).

33. Thomas Muller and Michael Fix, "The Impact of Selected Federal Actions on Municipal Outlays," prepared for the U.S. Congress, Joint

Economic Committee, 1979, pp. 84-87. This is a very important study, and its methodology is a model which future students of this subject will want to study closely.

34. United States Regulatory Council, *Regulation: The View from Janesville, Wisconsin and a Regulator's Perspective* (U.S. Regulatory Council, March 1980).

35. Advisory Commission on Intergovernmental Relations, *Categorical Grants: Their Role and Design* (Washington: USGPO, 1977), p. 237. See Richard B. Steward, "Pyramids of Sacrifice? Problems of Federalism in Mandating State Implementation of National Environmental Policy," *Yale Law Journal* 86 (1977):1196-1272, for a case study raising these concerns.

36. ACIR, *Categorical Grants,* p. 248.

37. Ibid.

38. 40 *C.F.R.* 6.200.

39. ACIR, *Categorical Grants,* p. 249.

40. Council of State Governments, *The Environment Comes of Age* (Lexington, Ky.: CSG, 1977), p. 12. CSG also notes that federal insistence on rigid deadlines for compliance undercuts the state's ability to bargain with industry in order to avoid legal action (p. 14).

41. 45 *C.F.R.* 80.

42. U.S. Department of Health, Education and Welfare, *A Summary of Information on the Costs to all HEW Grantees of Achieving Accessibility under Section 504 of the Rehabilitation Act* (HEW, July 11, 1979), pp. 5-6.

43. Congressional Budget Office, *Urban Transportation for Handicapped Persons, Alternative Federal Approaches* (Washington: USGPO, 1979). The Department of Labor, in estimating the average number of handicapped participants in its programs, found that only fourteen participants would use each of 376,198 program sites. Each facility would have to be modified to accommodate them in accordance with section 504 [45 *F.R.* 1404 (1980)].

44. National Governors' Association, *The Role of the Governor in the Implementation of Programs for the Handicapped* (Washington: NGA, 1979).

45. Arthur Anderson and Co., *Cost of Government Regulation Study.*

46. Charles T. Greene, CSP Chief of Occupational Safety and Health for the District of Columbia, *Testimony in U.S. House Subcommittee on Manpower and Housing, Occupational Safety and Health Administration—State Plans, Federal Agencies and Toxic Substance Identification, Hearings,* 95th Cong., September 14 and 19, 1978 (Washington: USGPO, 1979), p. 81.

47. U.S. House Subcommittee on Environmental, Energy, and Natural

Resources, *The Low-Income Weatherization Program in Connecticut: The Department of Energy Oversight, Hearings,* 96th Cong., December 14, 1979 (Washington: USGPO, 1980) pp. 5, 12, 20.

48. Copies of the correspondence are in the author's files.

49. James M. Taitt, "The Impact of Federal Regulatory Policies in the Environmental Arena: The Office of Surface Mining and West Virginia," paper delivered at the Southwestern Political Science Association, April 2-5, 1980, p. 10.

50. Ibid., pp. 10–11.

51. Ibid., p. 13.

52. For additional recommendations, see Edward I. Koch, "The Mandate Millstone," *The Public Interest* 61 (Fall 1980): 42–57.

2

Nationalizing State Policies

Mel Dubnick and *Alan Gitelson*

As we enter the 1980s, state and local governments find themselves in the midst of a major institutional upheaval. They are at the center of one of the most significant legal, administrative, and political changes to challenge U.S. government officials in this century. These have not been revolutionary changes, but instead have arisen since World War II in the subtle, incremental fashion typical of modern American politics and policymaking. They are not changes in the internal structures, procedures, or personalities of specific government entities, but rather in relations among them. They not only challenge the legal autonomy and constitutional authority of state and local units, but also their fiscal resources and administrative capacities. Most important of all, they are challenges to the fundamental roles that had evolved in the American federal system through the New Deal era.

To understand these changes and challenges, we must look to two simultaneous and closely related trends; the nationalization of American public policy and the increasing reliance on regulatory mechanisms by American policymakers. As separable developments, both trends are easy to document. The increasing role played by Washington in American public policy is indicated by both the growth of expenditures at that level and the rapid expansion of federal jurisdiction in a variety of domestic areas. Some of this growth and expansion involves issues previously outside the scope of all government levels (for example, nuclear power), but most reflects the escalation of policy responsibilities from state and local to national arenas (for example, highway speed limits and education).[1] The increasing application of regulatory solutions is indicated by the recent proliferation of both regulators and regulations, as well as a growing public and policymaker concern for the costs and changing nature of regulatory activity.[2] However, while each is important as an independent trend, the two combine to form an even more significant development: the *nationalization of regulatory policy*.

The nationalization of regulatory policy took root during the middle 1960s and gained momentum and substantive form during the 1970s. Traceable to the New Deal and the discovery of "national police powers," its more immediate sources are events surrounding Kennedy's New Frontier and Johnson's Great Society. During that period and its aftermath, the "positive national state and its programs" were accepted "as a positive virtue, as something desirable for its own sake and patently necessary for the society."[3] At first it emerged in efforts to guarantee and extend civil rights, but it was soon rationalized as acts necessary to protect the nation's public health and safety. By the 1970s, national regulatory efforts were commonplace in such issue areas as consumer protection, environmental protection, energy conservation, and economic stability.

State and local governments were not unaffected by this trend; in fact, they may have now become the principal vehicles through which nationalized regulations are instituted. This chapter examines the potential and actual roles played by subnational governments in the nationalization of regulatory activity and offers a descriptive framework for further analysis. The focus is on intergovernmental mechanisms in terms of both their form and long-range implications for American government. The basic theme directing this examination is that government regulations, like other public-sector services, are "deliverable" actions, and it is from this perspective that we begin.

Delivering Regulation

The nationalization of regulatory policy has had considerable impact on how governments operate *at all levels*. The means by which regulatory policy nationalization occurs can and have varied. The frequent assumption is that the nationalization of policy authority is directly related to the centralization of policy administration. This assumed correlation is inherent in a number of widely accepted theories used to explain the general trend toward nationalization.[4] The facts indicate otherwise, however, since there are numerous examples of policies involving the concentration of authority accompanied by decentralized implementation mechanisms. This is as true for regulatory policies as it has been for other forms of government activity in the United States. The difference is that the nationalization of regulatory policies is a relatively recent phenomenon, thus posing new situations and unique challenges for the American intergovernmental system and those who participate in it.

The simple distinction between policy formulation and implementation functions must be stressed at the outset if we are to understand the options available to policymakers charged with designing mechanisms for administering nationalized regulatory policies. Although often linked, these functions are structurally separable both analytically and in fact. Who formulates a policy and how that person (or persons) goes about the task are not necessarily correlated with a particular set of policy implementors or implementation procedures. It is on the basis of this premise that we can develop a typology of implementation mechanisms applicable to our analysis of nationalized regulatory policy.

An equally important premise is the view that regulations, like all government policies, can be perceived as *deliverable goods and services*. That is, it is not enough to regard a regulatory policy as a mere institution that has power just because it exists. Rather, a regulation, like a subsidy or service must be delivered. For present purposes, we assume a narrow definition of *regulation* by regarding it as a policy action by an authorized governmental agent imposing a specific standard of behavior on a target population under its jurisdiction.[5] Given this delineation, we can examine how regulations are delivered without presuming that officials promoting or authorizing the establishment or sanctioning of regulatory policy actions are identical to those authorized to carry them out.

The possibilities for nationalized regulatory policy implementation logically follow once these premises are accepted and placed within the context of the American federal system. These include situations in which

1. Both the authorizing and authorized units are national (*complete preemption*).
2. The authorizing entity is a state government, while the delivery of regulatory policy actions is national (*federalization*).
3. The national government authorizes or promotes the delivery of regulatory actions through interstate agreements or multistate organizations (*interstate organizations*).
4. The national government authorizes or promotes the delivery of regulatory actions through state and local governments (*intergovernmental relations*).

Of these four possibilities, only the first and fourth have been extensively used in the delivery of nationalized regulatory policies, and the first was of greater significance in the past than at present.

Federalization is an idea usually associated with proposals to reform the delivery of social-welfare policies. It is typically related to a fiscal crisis in states or cities and involves having national officials assume the responsibility for given policy functions at the behest of state and local officials.[6] In nationalized regulatory policy actions, an approach resembling federalization has been used, but generally only in emergency situations when state and local authorities have found conditions temporarily overwhelming. Examples are found mainly in activities involving immediate public health and safety problems, such as those associated with natural disasters or civil disorders. The sporadic, short-term, and localized nature of these efforts makes them unlikely models for more substantial long-term efforts to implement nationwide regulatory policy actions. On the one hand, it is unlikely that all states will simultaneously and of their own volition defer to national officials in policy areas where they retain legal authority to act. On the other hand, even if such mass deference was to occur, there is little like-lihood that a single national agency would be capable of carrying out its functions without having to mobilize state and/or local authorities in that effort. In such a situation, federalization would actually become merely a variation of the intergovernmental mechanisms that are being used to implement nationalized regulations.

Interstate organizations also are often proposed as mechanisms for implementing nationalized regulations, but they have in fact not been used in that role. Such mechanisms are rationalized on three grounds.[7] First, they would meet specific public problems at the appropriate *scale of effort*. That is, given problems may be of such nature that neither national nor state and local efforts would be relevant. Certain problems and their potential solu-tions may be technically regional in character, thus rendering interstate efforts as most appropriate.[8] In regard to this form of regulatory action, a regional approach to fighting water pollution in specific water basins or air pollution in contiguous areas would seem relevant.

Second, regional arrangements can facilitate the *administrative coordination* of national policies by bringing together relevant actors and resources at politically and economically more manageable levels.[9] As a possible means of implementing regulatory policy on a nationwide basis, these organizations could be used to plan and oversee the consistency of enforcement efforts by member units.

Third, regional organizations are often regarded as a means for *check-ing the tendency toward the centralization of power* while not barring nationalization of effort. Thus, while they permit the use of national resources in solving policy problems, they also decentralize the locus of national executive power through the establishment of distinct, functionally specialized, frequently autonomous government entities that can prove more flexible, adaptive, and open to regional interests and needs. Again, put in a regulatory-policy context, this type of arrangement could prove politically feasible and economically beneficial by accommodating regional variations on nationwide regulatory standards.

In operation, regional organizations have performed regulatory functions, but none are national in scope or impact. Most of these entities are primarily planning and coordinating bodies and thus perform no regu-latory tasks outside those administrative mandates they impose on their institutional members.[10] In the total picture of nationalized regulatory poli-cies they are not treated as special regional implementing mechanisms, but as variants of state and local jurisdictions. In short, they are regarded as participants in the intergovernmental system rather than as unique excep-tions to those relationships. As such they have not been utilized as a primary means for delivering nationwide regulations despite suggestions along those lines.[11] Nor is a change in this direction likely to prove politically or administratively feasible.[12] Regional organizations would be difficult to design on *a nationwide basis and even more difficult to operate* given the jurisdictional conflicts that inevitably arise. It is little wonder that this implementation mechanism for nationalized regulatory policies has not been utilized.

Complete preemption is not only more often applied, but also is the most significant one historically. On a formal and legal level, preemption involves the *national government's assertion and assumption of exclusive jurisdiction* over policy formulation and implementation functions in an issue area. As applied here, the idea of preemption is taken literally and is understood to entail the *complete* assumption of regulatory policymaking and policy implementation authority.[13] In this extreme form, preemption mandates that national officials *totally* occupy a "'field' to the exclusion of ... state action."[14]

In spite of its historical and constitutional significance, especially with respect to regulations rooted in the commerce power, the recent application of these preemptive mechanisms has been limited.[15] This is not to say that Congress has been reluctant to assert its authority in constitutionally preemptive terms. To the contrary, there have been a number of recent and significant legislative actions bluntly declaring it "to be the intent of Congress that the provisions of the Act shall supersede any and all laws of the States and political subdivisions thereof insofar as they may now or hereafter provide for. . . ."[16] However, among these acts there are few that have explicitly preempted *both* the power to formulate *and* the power to implement regulatory-policy actions. In most cases, the details of implementation and enforcement are either vaguely defined or else indicate a role for state or local governments in the implementation of the act.[17]

There is one major exception, but even that is limited in effect and qualified. Section 209(a) of the 1970 Clean Air Act expressly prohibits states or their subdivisions from adopting or attempting "to enforce any standard relating to the control of emissions from new motor vehicles or new motor vehicles' engines" subject to the act's motor vehicle emission and fuel standards. According to Lettie Wenner, this provision "constituted the first and only congressional mandate to the Environmental Protection Agency (EPA) to undertake directly enforcement of pollution controls without the assistance of state government.[18] However, there were several loopholes in this assertion of complete preemption. For one thing, states were given jurisdiction over the maintenance of these standards and related control devices once the vehicles were purchased and on the road. For another, the 1970 act contained a major exemption to the preemption. Termed the "California waiver," it authorized the state to impose more stringent controls.[19] Section 177 of the act as amended in 1977 extends this exemption to specially designated "nonattainment" areas.

The fourth and final group of delivery mechanisms for nationalized

regulatory policies are *intergovernmental*, and they are obviously the preferred option among the four types available to policymakers. At the heart
of intergovernmental mechanisms is the assumption that regulatory-policy
formulation and implementation are separable in fact as well as in theory.
However, relying on state, local, and even regional entities to administer a
set of nationally applicable regulations seems to violate several principles of
good management. The use of intergovernmental mechanisms would be an
open invitation to those seeking to qualify or subvert nationwide policy
actions, and some analysts have demonstrated that a "Gresham's Law of
Regulation" (that is, "less stringent regulations chase out more stringent
regulation") is evident in certain regulatory areas.[20] Yet, there are a number
of factors that can explain the tendency to place implementation responsibilities with lower-level jurisdictions.

First among these are the forces of history, particularly as these reflect
long-standing constitutional traditions. Despite the increasing trend toward
the nationalization of American public policy, there has rarely been any
serious consideration given to proposals to abolish states.[21] Local-government units have proven less sacrosanct and there have been some successful
(although hard fought) efforts toward metropolitan consolidation.[22] Tradition does not die easily, and this is as true of government functions (for
example, building codes, water-quality control, and highway traffic speed
limits) as it is of government jurisdictions. It is not surprising, therefore, to
find national policymakers deferring in part to states and localities by
allowing them to implement regulatory policies set in Washington.

A second and related factor is more ideological, for there exists a deeply
rooted bias within America's political culture favoring decentralized governance.[23] This belief in the value of state and local policymaking and policy
implementation may seem irrational or based on a number of potentially
questionable assumptions (for example, local governments are "more
representative," "more flexible and adaptable," more familiar with the
"needs and desires" of local populations), but it is nevertheless a force to be
contended with by policymakers and others involved in the design of nationalized regulatory policies. Under the influence of this bias, national policymakers are likely to minimize the degree of centralization either by providing for the participation of lower-level jurisdictions in the formulation of
regulatory policies or by leaving the administration of regulations to state
and local officials.

A third factor favoring the use of intergovernmental mechanisms is the
technical nature of the problems being regulated. There are certain subjects
of regulation calling for nationwide policy actions which nevertheless also
demand that regulatory treatments be adjusted to regional and local conditions. In energy conservation, for example, a national regulatory policy that
might call for new commercial buildings to achieve a minimum level of
energy efficiency would seem desirable in theory, but in practice would

prove extremely difficult to enforce. The technical benefits to be gained from relying on state or local officials are obvious. Standards appropriate to achieving national goals will differ from region to region and city to city given differences in geography, climate, and even economic and social conditions.[24] In the face of these variations the use of intergovernmental relations seems appropriate.

Related to technical factors are those rooted in the administrative capabilities, and fiscal resources of various levels of government are also factors favoring intergovernmental policy mechanisms. One commonly cited characteristic of America's federal system is the uneven distribution of those capabilities and resources. The national government has traditionally relied on transfer payments, grants-in-aid, and other forms of indirect policy implementation and has rarely established the organizations or a pool of trained personnel needed to carry out large-scale policy operations. It has offset this with a revenue-raising capacity that provides national policymakers with a substantial advantage over state and local officials. Taken together, these characteristics provide a powerful reason for Washington's reliance on lower-level jurisdictions to carry out a variety of national functions, including the delivery of nationalized regulatory policies.

Fifth and finally, political factors are an important determinant of the use of intergovernmental mechanisms. Viewing politics as the mobilization of bias, Schattschneider and others have indicated how political conflicts can be escalated or reduced as part of the tactics employed by interests involved in a policy debate.[25] The "privatization" or "socialization" of conflict is particularly relevant to political battles taking place within the American federal system. Simply put, an interest "losing" at one level or merely wishing to improve its standing in a political conflict can attempt to change from that level to another in a political conflict. Thus, if you are not getting your way at the state legislature, you might choose to raise the issue either locally in a city council or nationally in Congress. Given this perspective, one can explain the recent emergence of nationalized regulatory policies as a reflection of the increasing socialization of conflict from local, state, and nonpublic arenas to the national stage. Many activists—for example, environmentalists, consumer protectionists, Naderites—realized that theirs was a national constituency and that only by working in national policymaking arenas could they achieve their regulatory-policy objectives.[26] Simultaneously, however, there have been forces at work attempting to counter these efforts by seeking to privatize the conflict or otherwise reduce it to an issue involving lower-level jurisdictions. The typical result of this push and pull between socialization and privatization is a compromise in which a generally applicable policy is authorized by national officials, but with the stipulation that implementation would be left to state or local bodies.

The overall result of these five factors is a variety of intergovernmental delivery mechanisms for regulatory policies. The specific forms involved vary along two basic dimensions: (1) the extent to which lower-level jurisdictions participate of their own volition, and (2) the degree of discretion permitted to state and local officials in determining the specifics of a nationalized regulatory-policy action.

While the fundamental structure of the federal system (that is, national-state-local) lends itself to centralized organization and hierarchical relationships, in both constitutional theory and early historical practice the stress has been on noncentralized structures and fluid, pragmatically developed interactions among the many units making up the system.[27] Centralized and hierarchical tendencies have become increasingly evident in recent decades, but there remains a propensity among national policymakers to avoid overtly mandating state and local actions on behalf of national policy objectives. Therefore, one is likely to find that lower-level jurisdictions are often permitted a large degree of freedom in choosing to participate in the implementation of national policies. In other cases, the degree of choice is either nonexistent or merely symbolic. Between these extremes are the intergovernmental arrangements that either promote or constrain the options available to state and local officials in the face of national policy demands.[28]

The amount of substantive policy discretion allowed state and local officials will vary in a similar fashion. National regulations can be either specific or vague. In certain cases, the regulatory action or goal may be narrowly defined, and the substantive policy discretion allowed to states and localities is likely to be minimal. However, there are situations that allow state and local officials a considerable amount of choice in determining the objectives of regulatory actions and how they will be implemented. By issuing general guidelines for these policy efforts, national policymakers may seek their regulatory objectives while deferring to state and local decisions in most matters. As with the degree of volition, there is an almost infinite range of options for delivering nationalized regulatory policies.

These two dimensions are graphically correlated in figure 2-1. The resulting matrix illustrates the range of options available to policymakers in their efforts to deliver nationalized regulatory policies through intergovernmental mechanisms. An operational approach representative of each cell is provided in the figure, and the next section offers examples of each.

Four Intergovernmental Mechanisms

Technical Assistance: With Neither "Carrot" nor "Stick"

Each of the four representative mechanisms highlighted in figure 2-1 are distinctive not only because of the degree of volition and discretion they

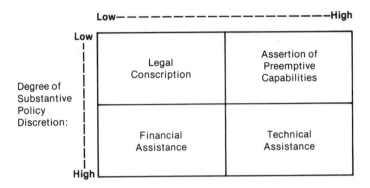

Figure 2-1. Degree of Volition Allowed Lower-Level Jurisdictions

allow state and local officials, but also because of the conditions they require for their effective application to specific regulatory-policy efforts. This is especially true for *technical-assistance* mechanisms. In its purest form, technical assistance involves neither the "carrot" nor the "stick," which is characteristic of the other three approaches to be discussed. By definition, technical assistance refers "to programs, activities, and services provided by the Federal Government, a Public Interest group, or another Third Party to strengthen the capacity of recipients to improve their performance with respect to an inherent or assigned function."[29] While this kind of assistance can be linked to a grant (or other form of aid) or perhaps even made mandatory through the imposition of sanctions, we are concerned with its use when unencumbered by "strings" in the form of either rewards or punishments.[30]

Technical assistance usually takes three forms.[31] First, it involves "general management assistance" aimed at helping recipient units build their capacity to deal with general-purpose government functions, for example, planning, budgeting, and staffing. Second, it takes the form of "technology transfer and sharing" programs that disseminate information that recipient units might find relevant and useful to their tasks. Finally, technical assistance can be used to deliver management and/or technical services (that is, "functional assistance") appropriate for specific programs or projects of the recipient government.

It is this last form of technical assistance that has been used to deliver nationalized regulatory policies. The surprising thing is that a form of functional assistance has been used quite successfully for this purpose since *at least* the turn of the century.

The primary example is the national standards of weights and measures implemented through state and local agencies by the Department of Commerce's National Bureau of Standards (NBS). National authorities in this particular area are given jurisdiction over uniform weights and measures by Article I, Section 8 of the U.S. Constitution, and the federal government has been active in this area through NBS and its predecessors since the early 1800s.[32] Yet this is a policy arena in which national regulatory standards are effectively delivered by state and local officials without the use of federal sanctions and with a great deal of discretion being left to lower-level jurisdictions regarding the details of implementation and enforcement.

At the heart of this system of regulatory-policy delivery are the technical services NBS provides for state and local officials. As the legally accepted reference for standard weights and measures, NBS derives considerable power from its acknowledged legitimacy on these matters. In addition, it has organized itself as a government laboratory ready to serve the needs of its clientele rather than as an enforcement agency ready to assert its constitutionally sanctioned authority. Through annual conferences on weights and measures it offers general advice and maintains its long-term functional dominance of the field. In case a unique or immediate problem arises, NBS is capable of mobilizing a team of highly trained scientists and technicians to develop solutions. And, all the while, the regulatory-policy actions that maintain a nationally uniform set of weights and measures are being delivered by state and/or municipal inspectors who are enforcing the statutes and codes of their own jurisdictions.

There seem to be three factors that make this approach viable. First, the subject of the regulatory effort is perceived as technical, therefore making functional assistance an appropriate channel for intergovernmental interaction. The less technical the subject is perceived to be, the more likely it is that state and local policymakers would be willing to interject their own values and priorities into the decision-making and implementation processes. Related to this is a second factor: the perceived legitimacy of those providing the services. This legitimacy can be built on grounds of either law or "expertness," or a combination of both. In weights and measures, NBS derives its legitimacy from both. On the one hand, through constitutional delegation and congressional action, NBS is empowered to be the sole determinant of national standards in this area. On the other hand, NBS's status and reputation as a "scientific" organization with unquestionable expertise in the field of weights and measures makes it the obvious resource for state and local officials working in this area. Third, the regulated activity should already be the subject of state and local government policies. In the absence of both federal carrots and sticks, the nationalization of regulatory policy through a voluntary mechanism such as technical assistance will succeed only where an operational unit is in place within recipient jurisdictions. NBS's job is made much easier, for example, by the fact that the regulation of commercial weights and measures is regarded as a common function of lower-level jurisdictions. Without a relevant state and local agency to implement these standards, NBS would have to turn to other arrangements or at least create appropriate state and local agents.

As a model for more recent efforts at nationalizing regulatory policy, the technical-assistance approach is being used again by NBS, this time with regard to building codes. The rationale for nationalizing building-code standards is both technical and political. Technically, it is possible—and for many officials, desirable—to develop a national system of effective performance standards regarding building structures and construction materials that can be adapted to specific regional and local needs. This has become possible because of advances in both communications and building technology that improve the dissemination of information and desirable because of the pressures derived from recent economic and energy crises. Politically, efforts to change local building codes are a manifestation of recent regulatory reform movements.[33] Increasing the role of performance standards in building codes would not only make these regulations less arbitrary, but would also help break the hold of local cartel-like arrangements in the construction industry. It would simultaneously promote innovation and help stimulate rehabilitation projects and energy-conservation experiments.

Whatever the specific reasons behind the nationalization of building-code standards, the use of technical-assistance mechanisms to implement them is well under way. However, of the three major conditions needed for the successful application of technical assistance in this implementation effort, only one is in place; that is, regulation through building codes is a common function of state and local governments. Whether these codes are perceived as technical issues and whether NBS's role is regarded as legitimate are the more important problems to be solved if this nationalization effort is to have a chance for success.

NBS has attempted to solve these problems through a strategy based on its statutory function to encourage, in cooperation "with other governmental agencies and with private organizations," the "establishment of standard practices, incorporated in codes and specifications."[34] Applying this general objective and utilizing its reputation as a primary "state-of-the-art" consultant on technical issue related to problems of measurement, NBS conducted a survey of the states in 1967 to ascertain their interest in establishing a "consortium of state building administrators" to deal with common issues of building regulation.[35] The response was positive, and NBS guided the creation of such an organization with technical assistance and administrative support. By December 1967, the National Conference of States on Building Codes and Standards (NCSBCS) was a reality. From 1968 to 1975, under NBS guidance, NCSBCS grew in size and influence as a regulatory delivery mechanism.[36]

In 1975, NCSBCS was incorporated as a separate nonprofit organization. NBS still provides a substantial amount of technical assistance to NCSBCS, and the two organizations jointly sponsor an annual conference on building regulations as well as other specialized meetings.[37] In short, the NBS-NCSBCS relationship is a firm and continuing one.

How effective has this NCSBCS strategy been in NBS's efforts to develop a nationally accepted building-code regulatory system through technical assistance? NCSBCS has been an effective vehicle for creating a sense of agreement among various state officials and the governments they represent. Its model acts and codes have drawn considerable attention and have been adopted in many jurisdictions. Working in conjunction with HUD, NCSBCS has played a central role in the Mobile Home Standards Enforcement Program, which is applied in many states. The energy crisis also has helped facilitate this implementation effort by enhancing the legitimacy of technically based building regulations in state and local conservation programs. Twenty-six states have already adopted NCSBCS's National Code for Energy Conservation in New Buildings, and with the technical assistance provided by NBS's National Engineering Laboratories, NCSBCS has developed a widely used Building Energy Performance Standards Program.

Extending these efforts to local governments provides an even greater challenge. In 1966, the Advisory Commission of Intergovernmental Relations estimated that approximately 8,000 government units had some form of building-code policy. Promoting statewide code adoptions is one tactic, but local circumstances—both political and technical—tend to make statewide solutions inappropriate or impossible. In the face of this, the technical-assistance approach has been applied to major local jurisdictions, and following the NBS model, NCSBCS has helped create and operate the Association of Major City Building Officials.

The jury is still out on these attempts to nationalize building-code regulations, but the preliminary verdict seems positive. No doubt the efforts of NBS are being aided by a variety of financial and legal programs operated through HUD, the Department of Energy, and related agencies. Nevertheless, this implementation approach does show promise as a distinctive mechanism useful under certain conditions that can attain national goals while imposing minimal burdens on lower-level jurisdictions.

Financial Assistance: The Tightening Strings

Intergovernmental relations are often based on fiscal ties among participating units. This financial link is so common and important that intergovernmental relationships are frequently defined as fiscal interactions.[38] Therefore, it is not surprising that the nationalization of regulatory policy has come to rely heavily on grants-in-aid and related mechanisms. The key to utilizing financial assistance is the attachment to grants of "strings" that reward or punish specific actions by recipient jurisdictions. Designing this system of carrots and sticks specifically to promote the implementation of nationalized regulations by state and local governments is the challenge.

The tools needed to meet this challenge are found among the great variety of mandates that accompany federal grants. For our purposes, a *mandate* "is any responsibility, action, procedure or anything else . . . imposed by constitutional, legislative, administrative, executive or judicial action . . . that is required as a condition of aid."[39] These mandates come in many forms, but again for our purposes we will focus on two characteristics: (1) what they require of recipients, and (2) the parameters of their application.

Mandates are either organizational/procedural or programmatic. Organizational/procedural mandates constituted most of the early forms of conditions attached to federal grants-in-aid and were originally regarded as a means for improving state and local governments rather than as a means for achieving certain national policy goals. Along these lines, receipt of federal funding depended on such things as reorganizing a recipient agency, hiring professionals, or the adoption of Civil Service personnel procedures in relevant program units. More recent mandates of this nature demand that recipient program units perform their tasks in a certain way, keep records and report about program activities in a certain fashion, hire and pay personnel according to a given set of rules, and carry out planning and evaluation functions. While these organizational/procedural mandates may ultimately affect what regulatory policies are adopted and enforced by state and local officials, they are not intended for that purpose. Rather, these are *administrative regulations* intended to influence the performance of government agencies and not the behavior of clientele groups or some other target population.

Programmatic mandate requirements, on the other hand, can result in state and local officials imposing a nationally designed or sanctioned regulation on a targeted group within a given jurisdiction. On a general level, these mandates can address three aspects of a required program or policy: first, that it exists (*program* mandates); second, that it be applied to a given quantitative level (*program quantity* mandates); and third, that it be of a certain quality (*program quality* mandates).[40] Thus a grant might require that a municipality have a public housing policy (program), that the policy generate x number of new public-housing units each year (program quantity), and that the units meet specified standards, such as location, type of occupancy—for example, family, elderly—and so forth (program quality). Applied to a regulatory-policy area such as building codes, a set of mandates might require that a municipality receiving HUD funds have a code (program), that the code's enforcement involve ten full-time inspectors (program quantity), or that it be based on performance standards set forth in a NCSBCS model code (program quality). It is through these programmatic requirements that mandates can be made effective vehicles for implementing nationalized regulatory policies.

The second dimension of mandates relevant to our discussion sets forth their application parameters. Simply put, mandates are either vertical or horizontal. *Vertical mandates* establish requirements within narrowly delineated policy areas. Thus, while a building code may be required by conditions laid out in a HUD urban renewal grant, the same requirement is unlikely to be found attached to a Law Enforcement Administration grant. *Horizontal requirements*, however, cut across often dissimilar and unrelated grant programs.[41]

Putting these two dimensions together in a matrix, we can illustrate the major forms these financial-assistance mechanisms can take. Figure 2-2 also specifies the examples for each cell, and these are briefly discussed in the following paragraphs.

An example of a *vertical program mandate* used to implement a national regulatory policy is the 1972 Coastal Zone Management Act.[42] Although the act itself affects only coastal states, section 303 makes it quite explicit that Congress intended it to be "the national policy . . . [t]o encourage and assist the States to exercise effectively their responsibilities in the coastal zone through the development and implementation of management programs to achieve the wise use of land and water resources. . . ."[43] Federal support for such state programs came in the form of grants to be issued under provisions set forth in Section 305 of the act. Those provisions call for recipient states to: (1) "identify the boundaries" of the zone subject to their program; (2) "identify land and water uses which have direct and significant impacts on coastal waters"; (3) inventory "geographic areas of particular concern"; (4) "develop broad guidelines on priorities of uses" within those areas; (5) "describe the organizational structure that will be used to implement the management program"; (6) "include a planning process that can identify public shorefront areas appropriate for increased access and/or protection"; (7) "include a planning process that can anticipate and manage the impacts from energy facilities in or significantly affecting the State's coastal zone"; (8) "include a planning process that can assess the effects of shoreline erosion . . ."; and (9) most relevant for our purposes, "identify the means by which they will exert control over land and water uses subject to the management program"[44]

In short, money was made available to recipient units *if* they would establish a coastal-zone management program and *if* that program included the *regulatory* means for dealing with coastal-zone issues. There are some

	Vertical	**Horizontal**
Program	Coastal Zone Management	Court-approved Desegregation plans
Program Quantity	Certificates of Need Program	10% minority business participation in public-works programs
Program Quality	55 m.p.h. maximum highway speed limit	Architectural barriers act requirements

Figure 2-2. Categories of Program Mandates

details provided, but only in very general terms.[45] One analyst described the act as little more than a "gentle nudge," and this is typical of most vertical-program mandate approaches; that is, they rely heavily on the willingness of potential recipients to participate, and when they do, there is considerable discretion left to state and local officials.[46] What differentiates these from technical-assistance strategies is the strong pull of financial aid. The carrot is offered as an inducement for voluntary action, thus rendering the degree of volition somewhat less than when the federal government does no more than makes technical services available.

Turning to *vertical program quantity mandates,* the federal Certificates of Need (CON) Program provides an example.[47] Under the National Health Planning and Resources Development Act of 1974, a CON Program was to be in place in every state by September 1980 using minimum standards set forth by HEW and implementation mechanisms organized on state and substate levels.[48] These standards were intended to help regulate and plan health-care delivery systems in ways that would improve the quality and distribution of such services while reducing aggregate costs. The type of minimum standards regarding substate needs was typically quantitative, with national guidelines permitting a distribution of certain health-care facilities (for example, intensive care units, CAT scanners) relative to the number, nature, and distribution of local populations. The "catch" was that while technically voluntary, states not complying with CON Program requirements would have Medicaid, child health care, and other health-care-related funding cut off. Thus in aid programs such as this there is a tendency for both the degrees of volition and discretion to be reduced—although the option not to participate or comply still exists.

The most obvious example of a *vertical program quality mandate* is the 55 mph maximum highway speed requirement attached to highway funding programs during the early 1970s. Highway funds, like all federal aid, are technically optional, particularly in the area of road maintenance. From the outset they have involved strings, but these have primarily been procedural or substantively technical (for example, materials to be used, engineering standards to be applied in designing roads, and so forth). The imposition of a specific national-program quality mandate such as the 55 mph speed limit constituted a major shift, for it involved a congressionally determined regulatory policy that was to be adopted and implemented by states *as their own*. To challenge this mandate was to risk losing access to a significant source of funding—a threat no state has been willing to test, although at least two (Wyoming and Oklahoma) have made gestures in that direction. The degrees of volition and discretion have proven extremely low in this instance.

Examples of horizontal or crosscutting mandates also reflect a variety of uses, some procedural and some substantive. Their application is based on the judicially accepted principle that the federal government "may properly attach terms and conditions to grants-in-aid to States, as long as such conditions are related to a legitimately national purpose and are not coercive."[49] Major horizontal mandate tools include Title VI of the 1964 Civil Rights Act, which forbids federal funding for organizations or government units that disciminate. This has been interpreted not only to make federal agency participation illegal, but also to make it the grantor's "affirmative duty" to monitor and prevent discriminatory actions by funded entities.[50] For the most part this has been an organization/procedural mandate, since the courts have narrowly defined Title VI to call for the termination of aid only to the specific program in which discriminatory action has been proven.[51]

In educational funding, however, the situation is different. If a recipient school district is lacking a court-approved desegregation plan, its funds may be cut off under Title VI provisions.[52] This use of Title VI as a *horizontal program mandate* has been at the heart of many confrontations both in and out of the courtroom. A *horizontal program quantity mandate* related to Title VI provisions is found in the 1977 Public Works Employment Act. That act requires that there be at least 10 percent minority business participation in the funded projects.[53] There are very few examples of *horizontal program quality mandates,* because national policymakers have been reluctant to create entire programs mandated for state and local adoption that use the threat of withholding federal assistance.[54] One example is found in provisions of the Architectural Barriers Act of 1968, which denies federal funds to any state or local agency that does not have an acceptable policy of accessibility for handicapped persons in all buildings and other public areas leased by the national government or whose construction is in part funded through Washington and for all "public conveyances" within their respective jurisdictions.[55]

There are many more instances of how intergovernmental financial-assistance mechanisms have been mobilized to implement nationalized regulatory policies.[56] These mechanisms also serve a variety of other purposes (administrative, political), and often alternative objectives take priority or otherwise contradict nationalization goals.[57] What we are witnessing, however, is a developing situation in which the national government's ability to use financial assistance to implement regulatory programs is gaining strength. State and local governments are becoming increasingly dependent on the many categorical and block grants generated in Washington, and there is some evidence that the priorities of officials at those levels are being reshaped by the programmatic opportunities they are offered.[58] Under conditions of fiscal stress, these tendencies are likely to be reinforced, and Washington's ability to fashion an effective intergovernmental delivery system for national regulations is going to improve in the process.[59]

Asserting Preemptive Capabilities: Using the Big Option

As noted earlier, complete preemption of a field by the national government is one major method for bringing about the nationalization of regulatory policy. In that instance we discussed the unqualified occupation of a field by Washington—a method used more in the past than at present. Nevertheless, a less than complete form of preemption continues to play a significant role today, but now in the context of intergovernmental strategies.[60]

The idea of using preemption to stimulate state and local participation in a nationwide policy system is not new. Its first major application as a delivery mechanism dates back to Washington's role in establishing an unemployment compensation system now in force in all fifty states. What is unique about that accomplishment is that all fifty states opted to join the system with full knowledge that federal officials would institute the policy if the state chose not to.[61]

The reasoning behind this approach is that if preemption gives national officials total jurisdiction over the formulation and implementation of a policy in a given field, then it also provides them with the ability to delegate their powers to lower-level jurisdictions if they so desire for purposes of carrying out national policy objectives. Formally this would involve (1) the legal assertion that the federal government was preempting state and local jurisdiction in a field, followed by (2) the development of a national program organized on a state-by-state basis, which includes (3) provisions and incentives for state and local assumption of all program responsibilities within their jurisdictions, with (4) the stipulation that these state or local programs meet a detailed set of structural, procedural, and substantive policy standards. Thus we have a system in which participation is highly voluntary but discretion is relative low.

A case in point is the Occupational Safety and Health Act (OSHA) of 1970, which asserts [section 2(b)] that it is the "purpose and policy" of Congress (under its commerce powers) "to assure so far as possible to every working man and woman in the Nation safe and healthful working conditions and to preserve our human resources. . . ."[62] State jurisdiction in such matters is technically preempted, and in section 6 the Secretary of Labor is given the responsibility for instituting national standards for occupational safety and health. Having established the legal supremacy of national authority in this field, the act goes on to provide two roles for the states. First, section 18 explicitly allows for state action in those areas where the Secretary had chosen not to promulgate rules and regulations. Second and more important, sections 18(b) and 18(c) (2) permit states to develop and enforce their own safety and health standards *if* they are at least as effective as the national standards established under section 6. Whether state programs meet this criterion is to be determined by the Secretary of Labor.

The incentives used to draw states into the OSHA system are set forth in section 23 of the act, and the emphasis is on providing financial assistance for states to study and plan for their involvement (up to 90 percent) followed by aid of up to 50 percent for the administration of a plan acceptable to the Secretary. This approach has proven only partly successful, for by 1977, only twenty-three states had processed approved plans, while interest among the others was waning.[63] This was a relatively poor performance in light of the complete acceptance of a similar option offered the states in the unemployment compensation programs set up under the 1935 Social Security Act. (In that instance, the incentive was tied into a tax-offset mechanism, and that would be difficult to apply in a regulatory program such as OSHA).[64] OSHA remains the primary example of this approach, but it is a delivery system coming into increasing use in areas such as strip mining and through judicial decisions having the effect of permitting state involvement in supposedly preempted issue areas.[65]

Legal Conscription: Toward Unitary Government

Of all the intergovernmental mechanisms used to nationalize regulatory policy, none is more revolutionary than the approach first applied in the Clean Air Act Amendments of 1970. It is an approach minimizing both the voluntariness of state and local participation and the substantive policy discretion provided for officials in subnational units. In fact, it is a mechanism that challenges the very essence of federalism as a noncentralized system of separate legal jurisdictions and instead relies upon a unitary vision involving hierarchically related central and peripheral units. It is an arrangement that goes beyond complete preemption or the assertion of preemptive capabilities. Rather it focuses political and administrative attention on national problems and assumes that policy solutions should determine the relationships among national and subnational governments. Using this logic, it is an approach allowing national policymakers and policy implementors to mobilize state and local resources on behalf of a national policy program. As preliminary measures, these resources can be mobilized using technical, financial, or other forms of assistance, but underlying this mechanism is the ability of national officials to formally and officially "draft" those resources into national service. We call this *legal conscription.*

As the first major use of this approach, the 1970 Clean Air Act (CAA) Amendments is a prime model for describing legal conspiration.[66] Ironically, the CAA begins [section 101 (a) (3)] by noting "that the prevention and control of air pollution at its sources is the primary responsibility of States and local governments. . . ." This declaration is immediately qualified [section 101 (a) (4)] by the finding "that Federal financial assistance and leadership is essential for the development of cooperative Federal, State, regional, and local programs to prevent and control air pollution." Given these grounds for action, section 107 (a) of the CAA asserts that each state *must* submit an "implementation plan" covering its "entire geographic area" and specifying "the manner in which national primary and secondary ambient air quality standards will be achieved and maintained within each air quality control region in such State." These implementation plans were to be based on air quality criteria and control techniques found to be acceptable by the administrator of the Environmental Protection Agency (EPA), who is also responsible for issuing the national ambient air quality standards to be adopted, maintained, and enforced by the states.[67] Moreover, if a state "fails to submit an implementation plan" meeting those standards, or if the EPA administrator finds a submitted plan unacceptable and the state does not meet EPA objections "within 60 days after notification," then the administrator "shall . . . promptly prepare and publish proposed regulations setting forth an implementation plan, or portion thereof, for a State. . . ."[68] Similar provisions [section 111(a) (2)] are also in place for national performance standards to be applied to "new stationary sources." Regarding enforcement, provisions in section 113 of the 1970 Clean Air Act make it clear that it is the responsibility of states to carry out the approved implementation plans, and if 30 days after notification by the

EPA administrator they do not enforce the plan, the EPA will take over such duties.

Other mechanisms are used in the 1970 Clean Air Act that are less demanding of states. We have already noted that (with exceptions) state involvement in new motor vehicle engine emission standards is completely preempted,[69] and the same holds true for aircraft emission standards.[70] In addition, there are certain provisions resembling the "assertion of preemptive capabilities" approach discussed earlier. Thus, according to section 112(d) (1), a state may, at its own volition but with the approval of EPA, implement and enforce emission standards for hazardous air pollutants. Similarly, a state can opt to participate in the inspection and monitoring of emission sources if its plan for this participation is approved.[71] However, in neither instance does this mean that the administrator cannot assert EPA's authority to carry out those tasks. Finally, section 105 of the Clean Air Act does make use of financial-assistance mechanisms by authorizing the administrator to offer aid of from 50 percent to two-thirds of the cost of planning, improving, and maintaining of air pollution control programs. Nor did the Act cut off all policy input for the states in those areas in which it applies legal conscription. Very prominent in the act is section 116, which states that, except where noted, nothing in the legislation "shall preclude or deny the right of any state or political subdivision thereof to adopt or enforce" a regulation that is *at least as stringent* as those provided by EPA.

In spite of these exceptions, the 1970 act represents a major alteration in national-subnational relations. The unitary system it assumes shows up most clearly in sections dealing with ambient air quality standards and performance standards set for new stationary sources. The precedent it sets has not gone unfulfilled. Major modifications of the act in 1974 and 1977 failed to make any significant changes in these provisions and, in fact, may have further enhanced them.[72] These mechanisms also were used in the Federal Water Pollution Control Act Amendments (FWPCAA) of 1972.[73] In fact, many FWPCAA provisions seem a direct copy of those in the CAA. In section 402(c), for instance, the act requires that all permits granted by the states under the National Pollution Discharge Elimination System (also established by FWPCAA) must comply with national minimum standards. Another case in point is section 303 of FWPCAA, which stipulates that states may adopt water quality standards of their own in addition to those set forth by the EPA administrator, but (as in CAA) these must be reviewed and approved by EPA to ensure that they are at least as stringent as the national standards.

An even more significant adoption of the legal-conscription approach is found in the 1978 National Energy Policy Acts. For example, section 212 of the National Energy Conservation Policy Act (NEPCA) mandates that the

Department of Energy (DOE) establish standards for the safety, effectiveness, and installation of energy conservation efforts, and that these be incorporated in state residential energy conservation plans that *must* be submittted by the governor of each state within a specified time.[74] If no such plan is forthcoming or found acceptable, DOE's Secretary is authorized under section 219 to promulgate and implement such a plan. Similarly, the legal-conscription approach is used in Title III of NECPA, which mandates state plans for energy conservation programs in schools, hospitals, and other public buildings. If a state plan fails to get Washington's approval, the Secretary may issue and force implementation of a DOE plan.

While legal-conscription mechanisms are "on the books," they have seen rather limited use. For a variety of reasons which we will not go into here, national policymakers and policy implementors are likely to prefer less coercive and more indirect approaches—those which provide either greater discretion or volition for state and local officials. Yet legal conscription is a potentially powerful tool for national officials to use, and in the case of environmental protection, we may see greater reliance on it in the near future. For the moment, however, it is only a "high explosive" in the arsenal of intergovernmental mechanisms that can be used to nationalize regulatory policies.

Implications

As a major trend in American public policy, the nationalization of regulatory policy can be easily documented. In this chapter we have focused on one aspect of that trend which might, in the long term, prove even more significant than the nationalization process itself: the increasing utilization of intergovernmental mechanisms to deliver those regulatory actions.

The implications of this development will, of course, have a direct influence on regulatory efforts. There can be little doubt that the effectiveness and efficiency of public-sector actions to achieve policy objectives through regulation will be affected by the choice of an intergovernmental delivery mechanism. Under certain conditions, the use of these mechanisms may prove technically and administratively justified. For instance, where regulated acts or conditions vary from location to location, it might prove beneficial to leave the specific context of nationally sponsored regulations to the judgment of state or local officials. And even where local circumstances do not warrant such discretion, the distribution of available human and financial resources among jurisdictions may mandate that subnational officials undertake various administrative responsibilities associated with a given set of regulatory policies. In most cases, however, the fact that intergovernmental approaches prove appropriate and relevant seems more the result of fortuitous coincidence than of calculated design.[75] Were it possible to associate the effectiveness and efficiency of a regulatory-policy endeavor with a particular intergovernmental delivery mechanism, the possibility of designing nationwide regulations would be enhanced. For that reason alone it might be fruitful to investigate the immediate policy implications of the four mechanisms.

However, it is the systematic implications that will ultimately prove more interesting, for the growing reliance on these intergovernmental mechanisms will inevitably take its toll on America's political institutions and relationships. The major dimensions of these systemic implications are threefold: fiscal, political, and legal/constitutional. In this brief conclusion we will touch on each implication both in terms of its actual impact and in terms of potential effects it might have in the near future.

Fiscal Implications

In the current period of fiscal stress and economic "stagflation," the past behavior of governments seems perverse and almost self-destructive. We often forget how comfortable we were as an affluent society and how satisfied we were with a policy system that distributed and even redistributed rather than regulated. We have come from a time when intergovernmental relations were truly "cooperative," when the relationships among federal, state, and local units were essentially "fiscally facilitative." That is, until recently, intergovernmental relations were marked by two fundamental characteristics: first, they were primarily based on financial assistance, with funds flowing from the center to peripheral units; and second, when conditions were attached to that assistance, they were typically designed to enhance subnational (as opposed to national) policy objectives and program implementation.[76]

While recipient units might have felt at times that the organizational/procedural strings and mandates attached to many grants were arbitrary and bothersome, these requirements were rarely intended as means for "controlling" state and local officials or making them mere agents of the national government. But all this changed in the middle 1960s, specifically with the passage of the 1964 Civil Rights Act. This early period witnessed a shift in national policymaker intentions, for from that time forward there has been a growing tendency to use intergovernmental relations as a means for asserting national control over state and local policies.

A second and related development emerged during the recent period of fiscal conservatism. This past decade has been characterized by budget cuts, "sunset" laws, deregulation programs, Proposition 13's, and associated retreats from "distributive politics." It also has witnessed an increasing propensity on the part of national officials to rely on regulation rather than spending and the delegation of authority rather than the acceptance of responsibility. The result has been twofold: first, an intergovernmental system that is more capable of imposing national policy requirements on subnational actors; and second, a declining reliance on financial assistance alone to accomplish that control. The fiscal implications of utilizing each intergovernmental mechanism must be examined within the context of these developments.

Generating state and local cooperation through technical-assistance programs alone is, as we have noted, a rarely used approach. For an agency such as NBS to successfully nationalize building-code regulations, there must exist the right combination of time, technical policy conditions, resources, and personnel. Obviously, when these conditions are all present, the technical-assistance approach promises to have minimal impact on government spending. Creating and maintaining the intergovernmental organizations (for example, NCSBCS) and relationships needed to carry out the assistance program would call for adjustments in expenditures by governments at all levels, but these would prove relatively insignificant.

Where optimal conditions do not exist, however, the technical-assistance strategy for nationalizing regulatory policies will have to be supplemented with alternative mechanisms. Using the building-code example, financial assistance can be made available to those jurisdictions needing help in developing the necessary infrastructures or training programs that would make it possible to participate in the technical-assistance effort. This is, in fact, an ingredient in the current NBS-NCSBCS strategy. It also might be possible for NBS to assert its preemptive capabilities in the area of standard setting as a means for imposing a basic building code that states and localities could build upon if they wished. This could prove a costly proposition whether or not subnational officials opted to participate in such a program. The same would hold for a strategy in which state and local participation in a nationwide building-code system was legally prescribed. In short, while technical-assistance mechanisms can deliver nationalized regulatory policies with relatively minimal economic and fiscal implications for state and local governments, creating the right conditions for such assistance could prove very costly.

Except in situations where existing state or local policies already meet national requirements, the use of the other three intergovernmental mechanisms is likely to increase the costs of government operations. Where their respective impacts will differ is in the distribution of those costs. A delivery strategy relying on legal conscription alone will obviously place the burden almost entirely on subnational units. The distribution of costs under the "assertion of preemptive capabilities" approach will depend on the role state and local units choose to play in the regulatory effort given their options. In either instance there is bound to be considerable pressure to modify the costly implications of each approach, and it is in this context that we see why financial assistance had proven to be the most commonly utilized mechanism. Faced with demands mandated by a system of legal conscription, state and local officials will lobby long and hard for fiscal assistance to help offset the costs of their participation.[77] And faced with the state and local reluctance to get involved in regulatory programs where they have an option, federal officials are likely to include substantial financial incentives in national programs.

However, financial-assistance programs, whether used as the primary mechanism for nationalizing regulatory policies or as a supplement to other approaches, have their own limitations and drawbacks. For one thing, as the "balanced budget" and "Proposition 13" mentality spreads from lower-level jurisdictions to Washington, the funding available for financial assistance of any kind may become more problematic. Under such conditions, national officials charged with carrying out regulatory mandates might feel compelled to rely more heavily and directly on legal conscription or any of the other mechanisms at their disposal. The fiscal burdens may therefore end up at the subnational level regardless of the current high reliance on financial assistance.

Assuming that the federal government's financial capabilities are not reduced in the future, there remain several drawbacks that can have significant implications for the fiscal condition of recipient units. These drawbacks emerge from the ever-expanding number and scope of fiscal-assistance programs, and not merely those associated with nationalized regulatory actions. The lure of federal grants is substantial, for they enhance state and local capabilities to provide more services and undertake new activities in areas that would go unserved without the availability of outside funding. The attractiveness of community development block grants and categorical assistance for water quality control, mass transit, law enforcement, flood control, and similar programs cannot be overstated. Nor can we stress too much the political and economic pressures on eligible subnational units to take advantage of these opportunities. The carrots are much too inviting, and besides there is the feeling that "If we don't take it [federal grants], someone else will."[78]

Problems arise, however, because of the distorting effects these grants produce in state and local activities. Levine and Posner have noted at least six such distortions: (1) the erosion of budgetary flexibility in subnational units; (2) the distortion of overall budgetary and program priorities within recipient entities; (3) the tendency to "protect" federally funded programs first; (4) increasing intraorganizational, interagency, and intergovernmental conflicts over policy and program priorities; (5) increasing deference to the federal determination of local problems; and (6) reductions in local planning and coordination.[79]

The adverse implications of these developments are not merely predictions, for they are having considerable influence right now. The distorting effects of financial-assistance mechanisms were brought home to New York City officials in their effort to cut back expenditures during their recent fiscal crisis. They found so much of their spending tied to federal aid "matching fund" programs that they were forced to focus their reductions in police, fire, sanitation, and other basic "housekeeping" functions where federal grants did not mandate major cutbacks. In the meantime, "special" programs that were linked to federal funding tended to survive.[80]

A less dramatic and perhaps more typical example is the experience of Lompoc, California. There a federal grant for the development of flood and water control will prevent the accumulation of storage of much needed water resources for this community during its long dry season.[81] Clearly, the possibility of a large federal grant was too inviting a carrot for the local city council and manager to ignore, and as the number of such opportunities increases, some very mundane yet critical choices will be made regarding local government priorities. Ultimately these choices will be reflected in fiscal patterns that might prove as significant for Lompoc and similar jurisdictions as New Yorks' past decisions did for it.

Of course, the *actual* fiscal implications of relying primarily on financial assistance or any other delivery mechanism could prove positive. Moreover, even where adverse impacts arise, these must be weighed against the productive and beneficial side of each effort.

Political Implications

At first glance the nationalization of regulatory policies through intergovernmental mechanisms would seem to have rather obvious political implications, that is, an increase in the relative power of national over subnational units. Nationalization necessarily implies state and local deference to Washington, and it would logically follow that national officials have the potential leverage to work their will on lower-level jurisdictions through the manipulation of technical, financial, or legal resources. This has led one local official to describe himself and others in his situation as the intergovernmental systems' "grunts." A *grunt* is defined as a low-skilled, poorly qualified worker requiring the most supervision. "In short, you have to keep the grunt on a short string." He goes on to describe the grunt's perspective as analogous to that of a "drunk's" view of a Salvation Army soup kitchen—we'll take their religion as long as we can get our bellies warmed."[82] In such a subordinated and subservient position, the local official appears relatively powerless, a victim of centralized power who must defer to survive. The label best summarizing this situation is Michael Reagan's "permissive federalism," that is, an intergovernmental relationship in which subnational units function in areas and ways that national officials permit them to function.[83]

A contrasting image also can be made, one that focuses on the considerable political leverage state and local officials gain from involvement in a variety of national regulatory efforts.[84] The various intergovernmental arrangements developed for carrying out federally sanctioned or promoted policies have one thing in common: they generally make subnational officials part of a national program. Within specific programs where state or local officials are provided some discretion concerning the content or administration of a national policy, the power of lower-level jurisdictions is greatly enhanced. This is the case in pesticide regulation, which is coordinated by EPA but implemented in many major farm states by agencies (for example, departments of agriculture) that are likely to prove less stringent in both their standards and enforcement.[85]

State and local officials also can obtain considerable political leverage over some national programs because of the roles they play in other intergovernmental capacities. Thus governors who wish to influence national energy policies in their states can mobilize the resources put at their disposal by Congress (and EPA) through environmental legislation, and vice versa. Or a city manager can significantly delay or adjust federal highway construction plans by activating provisions of environmental acts or the historical preservation requirements mandated in many grant programs. Here the image is not that of grunts, but of Machiavellians capable of using resources at their disposal to manipulate the system for desired ends. The significant point is that many of these resources are derived from the leverage state and local officials obtain from being part of the intergovernmental arrangements used to deliver nationalized regulatory policy actions.

Therefore it would be difficult to draw any straightforward conclusions regarding the political implications of our four delivery mechanisms. A great deal depends on whether the subnational official involved takes on the qualities of a grunt or a Machiavellian. Some generalizations can be offered, however. For example, those mechanisms characterized by high volition (that is, technical assistance and the assertion of preemptive capabilities) provide greater leverage and opportunities for Machiavellian behavior than those marked by lower volition. Among financial-assistance mechanisms, block grants and general revenue-sharing programs will facilitate more leverage for recipient units than categorical grants. Moreover, while it might prove more difficult to gain leverage in a situation where legal conscription is the principal vehicle for delivering nationalized regulatory policies, the payoffs (in terms of increased political power) are likely to prove extremely valuable for subnational officials who learn how to utilize their positions in the nationalized regulatory policy system.

In short, as with fiscal implications, it is difficult to predict the political impact of using any of these four intergovernmental delivery mechanisms. The only thing that can be said with certainty is that there will be some political effects. What they will be, however, remains an empirical question.[86]

Legal/Constitutional Implications

If there is one area where the potential impact of these alternative delivery mechanisms seems reasonably clear, it is first, the question of any government's legal right to regulate in given areas; and second, the question of federalism and intergovernmental relationships. On the first point, there can be little doubt of government's legal standing to pursue regulatory programs in the areas of new or social policies (for example, occupational safety and health, environmental quality, energy usage, and so forth). Many of these have not traditionally been associated with national policy actions, but a perusal of early urban and state records indicates that government actions in these areas are historical facts. Generally falling under the rubric of police powers, government activities in these arenas have only recently been taken up in Washington. Nevertheless, they have been and remain legally relevant matters for governments to deal with.

Somewhat more controversial is the second issue of jurisdictional responsibilities and the condition of American federalism. In a formal and theoretical sense, federalism and intergovernmental relations are separable concepts. One might regard all federal relations as being intergovernmental, but not all intergovernmental relations as being federal. Taking the formal definition, *federalism* is a nonhierarchical, noncentralized pattern of interactions among member units in an organization. Ideally it is a system that operates on a principle of conflict among member units that can be resolved only through negotiations and the development of an acceptable consensus to which disagreeing units can consent. This *conflict-consent model* is in contrast to a unitary system in which a single dominant unit renders a decision that is imposed on subordinated units. The subordinates should defer to the leading entity and cooperate in carrying out its mandates. Reluctance to cooperate is met with coercive sanctions. This is called a *cooperative-coercive model.*[87]

Of the four intergovernmental mechanisms examined here, only technical assistance seems to avoid a tendency toward unitary organization. The federal bias is a strong ingredient in the decision to rely totally or primarily on technical aid. The idea that national officials might be entrusted to activate this approach is evident in the case of NBS-NCSBCS. Even more significant is NBS's use of this mechanism in the area of weights and measures, since it is obvious from a reading of the Constitution that Congress can easily and quite legally assert its preemptory capabilities in that area. In areas of less explicit constitutional delegations, this approach would seem even more inviting *if* the right conditions were in place.

In certain cases, financial assistance also complements the federal bias. The greater the degree of volition and policy discretion permitted grant recipients, the more relevant the conflict-consent model becomes. However, in delivering nationalized regulatory mandates, financial-assistance mechanisms are unlikely to be very loose along either dimension. The 55 mph maximum highway speed requirement may not be typical, but it reflects the overall direction and form of grant programs as a means for producing changes in state and local regulatory policies. The cooperation-coercion image is obviously more relevant in such cases.

When national officials choose to formally assert their preemptive capabilities in an issue area, they are likely to be moving in the direction of unitary arrangements while maintaining some semblance of federalism. The latter emerges in the options that national officials allow subnational governments, but even here the federal bias is extremely limited. In OSHA, for example, states have the option to either take part in a unitary national regulatory system or retain their independence by avoiding any activities in those matters that OSHA chooses to address.

However, it is in legal-conscription mechanisms that the movement away from traditional federalism is both most blatant and extreme. By being able to use its legal capacities to literally force subnational units to act on behalf of national policies, Washington takes on the role of a hierarchical superordinate that can use coercive sanctions to compel cooperation from state and local units.

Legally and constitutionally this can only be described as a revolutionary change in formal American government institutions. It is a change that has been obscured both by our tendency to use the terms *federalism* and *intergovernmental relationships* interchangeably and by the propensity for policymakers and implementors to rely directly and primarily on financial assistance. Legal conscription, like the abstract set of relations we call *federalism*, is intergovernmental, but of an entirely different breed. As we witness a movement toward it and the assertion of preemptive capabilities (as well as a simultaneous movement away from financial and technical assistance), we are witnessing one more step in the ongoing demise of traditional federal relationships. Some might welcome this, others not. The point is, however, that the choices made among the available intergovernmental delivery mechanisms have more than immediate, short-term consequences. The implications can prove much more radical and enduring in constitutional as well as fiscal and political terms.

Notes

1. See Theodore J. Lowi and Alan Stone (eds.), *Nationalizing Government: Public Policies in America* (Beverly Hills, Calif.: Sage, 1978), especially Lowi's "Europeanization of America? From United States to United States." In another context Lowi asserts that perhaps 90 percent of the functions addressed by federal action today were almost exclusively within the jurisdiction of the states prior to the nationalization trend; see his *American Government: Incomplete Conquest* (Hilsdale, Ill.: Dryden Press 1976), p. 135.

2. See William Lilley III and James C. Miller III, "The New 'Social Regulation'," *The Public Interest* 47(Spring 1977), especially table 1, p. 50. Also see "Interventionist Government Came to Stay," *Business Week,* September 3, 1979, p. 39. On the general costs of government regulation, see Murray L. Weidenbaum and Robert DeFina, *The Cost of Government Regulation of Economic Activity,* reprint No. 88 (Washington: American Enterprise Institute for Public Policy Research, 1978). For a summary of relevant cost studies, see Lee Dymond, Donald Zimmerman, and Terrance Davey, "Costs and Benefits of Regulation: A Survey of Studies," in *Regulatory Reform Seminar: Proceedings and Background Papers* (Washington: Office of Regulatory Economics and Policy, U.S. Department of Commerce, 1978), appendix A. The changing "nature" of regulation has been described in a number of ways. Lilley and Miller, p. 53, distinguish between the "old" economic regulation and the "new" social regulation. Paul H. Weaver makes a similar distinction between older regulations which reflected the values of the populist-progressive movement, and the newer regulations emerging from the values of a "new class"; see his "Regulation, Social Policy, and Class Conflict," in Chris Argyris et al. (eds.), *Regulating business: The Search for an Optimum* (San Francisco: Institute for Contemporary Studies, 1978). Still another analysis sees the shift from regulatory policies which sought to *facilitate* the activities of target populations to contemporary regulations which seek to *control* those activities; see Melvin J. Dubnick and Lafayette Walker, "Problems in U.S. Standard-Setting: The Implications of the Shift to Control Functions," *Midwest Review of Public Administration* 13(1):25–49.

3. Lowi, Theodore J. "Europeanization of America?" in *Nationalizing Government* (1978), pp. 17–18.

4. One finds this assumption, for example, in a variety of "developmental" theories of economic growth (for example, those associated with Adolph Wagner, Alan T. Peacock and Jack Wiseman, and W.W. Rostow); see Bernard P. Herber, *Modern Public Finance: The Study of Public Sector Economics,* 3rd ed. (Homewood, Ill.: Irwin, 1975), pp. 366–375. Discussions of the centralizing pull of technological developments also tend to

assume the correlation of authority and implementation; see Samuel H. Beer, "The Modernization of American Federalism," *Publius* 3(2):74–80. The "traditional paradigm" of public administration includes a normative bias along these lines; see Vincent Ostrom. *The Intellectual Crisis in American Public Administration,* rev. ed. (Univ. of Alabama Press, 1974).

5. This "policy action" perspective is different from those relying on "institutional" or "functional" views of regulation; see Mel Dubnick, "Making Regulators Regulate," paper presented at 1979 National Conference on Public Administration, Baltimore, Maryland. Governments often authorize private entities to regulate themselves or others under a contractual arrangement (that is, self-regulation), but for present purposes we will limit our analysis to regulations carried out by government agencies.

6. This approach to social-welfare reform was initially presented in a June 1966 report issued by HEW's Advisory Council on Public Welfare ("A Nationwide Comprehensive Program Based upon a Single Criterion: Need"): for more background, see Daniel P. Moynihan, "The Crisis in Welfare," in *Coping: Essays on the Practice of Government* (New York: Random House, 1973).

7. For an indepth discussion of interstate and regional organizations, see Martha Derthick and Gary Bombardier, *Between State and Nation: Regional Organizations of the United States* (Washington: Brookings Institution, 1974), especially chapter 1.

8. This is the rationale behind several major interstate authorities: the Tennessee Valley Authority, the Delaware River Basin Commission, and the Appalachian Regional Commission.

9. "Coordination" functions are the primary reasons underlying the creation of several interstate organizations developed under Title V of the 1965 Public Works and Economic Development Act: Coastal Plains, Four Corners, Ozarks, and Upper Great Lakes Commissions.

10. For example, Title V commissions and various entities created under Title II of the 1965 Water Resources Planning Act, see Derthick and Bombardier, *Between State and Nation,* p. 7.

11. Frank P. Grad, "Intergovernmental Aspects of Environmental Controls," in *Managing the Environment* (Washington: U.S. Environmental Protection Agency, November 1973), pp. 323–349.

12. See conclusions reached in Derthick and Bombardier, *Between State and Nation,* chapter 11.

13. See Harrop A. Freeman, "Dynamic Federalism and the Concept of Preemption," *DePaul Law Review* 21(1972):630–648.

14. Samuel Krislov, "The Supreme Court in the Political Process," in Daniel J. Elazar et al. (eds.), *Cooperation and Conflict: Readings in American Federalism* (Itasca, Ill.: Peacock, 1969), p. 157. The national government's ability to mobilize preemptive mechanisms is found primarily

in specific passages of the Constitution; for a brief overview, see James B. Croy, "Federal Supersession: The Road to Domination," *State Government* 48(1):32-36. However, preemption also has emerged through court decisions not directly linked to those passages, for example, whenever significant conflicts arose between national policies and state actions; see Freeman, "Dynamic Federalism."

15. See C. Herman Pritchett, *The American Constitution,* 2d ed. (New York: McGraw-Hill, 1968), chapter 14.

16. Croy, "Federal Supersession," p. 33.

17. York Willbern, "The States as Components in an Areal Division of Powers," in Arthur Maass (ed.), *Area and Power: A Theory of Local Government* (Glencoe, Ill.: Free Press), p. 71. For example, the 1964 Civil Rights Act contains clearly preemptory declarations of state and local activity in the area of civil rights while simultaneously mandating state and local efforts to carry out national policy wishes in these areas. Thus the act outlaws any discriminatory policy actions required by state law or "carried on 'under color of the law' or 'any custom or usage required or enforced by officials of the state.'" See Pritchett, *The American Constitution,* pp. 729 and 736. This is not atypical of the approach taken by national policymakers in many regulatory areas; that is, preemptive terminology is used but never actually intended.

18. Lettie McSpadden Wenner, *One Environment Under Law: A Public Policy Dilemma* (Pacific Palisades, Calif.: Goodyear, 1976), p. 90.

19. See James E. Krier and Edmund Ursin, *Pollution and Policy: A Case Essay on California and Federal Experience with Motor Vehicle Air Pollution, 1940-1975* (Berkeley, Calif.: Univ. of California Press, 1977).

20. C.K. Rowland and Roger M. Marz, "Interstate Inequities in the Implementation of Toxic Substance Regulations: The Case of Pesticides," paper presented at December 1979 Symposium on Regulatory Reform, Chicago, Illinois.

21. Such proposals have been primarily academic, for example, Roscoe C. Martin, *The Cities and the Federal System* (New York: Atherton, 1965), p. 76.

22. See Elinor Ostrom, "Metropolitan Reform: Propositions Derived from Two Traditions," *Social Science Quarterly* 53(December 1972): 474-493.

23. See Anwar H. Syed, *The Political Theory of American Local Government* (New York: Random House, 1966).

24. For example, Ronald D. Brunner, "Decentralized Energy Policies," *Public Policy* 28(1):71-91.

25. E.E. Schattschneider, *The Semisovereign People: A Realist's View of Democracy in America* (New York: Holt, Rinehart and Winston, 1960); also see Roger W. Cobb and Charles D. Elder, *Participation in American*

Politics: The Dynamics of Agenda Building (Baltimore: Johns Hopkins University Press, 1972); and Robert Eyestone, *From Social Issues to Public Policy* (New York: Wiley, 1978).

26. See Mark V. Nadel, *The Politics of Consumer Protection* (Indianapolis: Bobbs-Merrill, 1971); also Paul Sabatier, "Social Movements and Regulatory Agencies: Towards A More Adequate—and Less Pessimistic—Theory of 'Clientele Capture,'" *Policy Sciences* 6(3):301–342; and Jeffrey M. Berry, *Lobbying for the People: The Political Behavior of Public Interest Groups* (Princeton, N.J.: Princeton Univ. Press, 1977).

27. Daniel J. Elazar, *American Federalism* (N.Y.: Crowell, 1972); also Parris N. Glendening and Mavis Mann Reeves, *Pragmatic Federalism: An Intergovernmental View of American Government* (Pacific Palisades, Calif.: Palisades Publishers, 1977).

28. For a potentially useful typology of middle-range approaches, see David L. Weimer, "Federal Intervention in the Process of Innovation in Local Agencies: A Focus on Organizational Incentives," *Public Policy* 28(1):93–116.

29. This Office of Management and Budget Policy Study Committee definition is cited in *State and Local Governments' Views on Technical Assistance, A Staff Study,* issued by the General Accounting Office on July 12, 1978 (pp. 1–2).

30. See Paul J. Flynn, James D. Carroll, and Thomas A. Dorsey, "Vertical Coalitions for Technology Transfer: Toward an Understanding of Intergovernmental Technology," Publius 9(3):3–33.

31. General Accounting Office, *State and Local Governments' Views on Technical Assistance* (Washington: USGPO), pp. 2–3.

32. Rexmond C. Cochrane, *Measures for Progress: A History of the National Bureau of Standards* (Washington: U.S. Department of Commerce, 1966), chapter 1.

33. Scandals have long plagued this field, and it is usually regarded as a prime example of "capture" and "producer protection" regulation, wherein some special interests (in this case, plumbers, carpenters, and other members of the building trades) are served rather than the "public health, safety, and welfare."

34. Cited in *C.F.R.* 200.100(a) (4).

35. *C.F.R.* 200.104(a).

36. Among other accomplishments, it has issued model state legislation and regulations on such matters as mobile homes, manufactured buildings, statewide building codes, and the registration of enforcement officials. It developed a system for accrediting evaluation testing laboratories and established formal and informal operational linkages between itself and other relevant private and public organization (for example, the American Society for Testing and Materials, the National Institute of Building Sciences, the Building Seismic Safety Council).

37. The relationship was further enhanced by the activities and career of NCSBCS's first chairman, Gene A. Rowland, who later became chief of NBS's Building Research Division and director of its Office of Engineering Standards. In short, there exists strong personal ties that have added to NCSBCS's success as an NBS strategy. See, "A Brief Overview of NBS-NCSBCS Research and Assistance to the Building Community," in *Research and Innovation in the Building Regulatory Process,* NBS Special Publication 552 (Gaithersburg, Md.: U.S. Department of Commerce, National Bureau of Standards, July 1979), pp. 5-12. The authors would like to thank Lafayette Walker of NBS for his help in this research.

38. See Deil S. Wright, *Understanding Intergovernmental Relations: Public Policy and Participants' Perspectives in Local, State, and National Governments* (North Scituate, Mass.: Duxbury Press, 1978), pp. 8-14.

39. Catherine Lovell, "The Mandate Issue," in Catherine Lovell et al. (eds.), *Federal and State Mandating on Local Governments: An Exploration of Issues and Impacts* (Riverside, Calif.: Graduate School of Administration, University of California, June 1979), p. 32. The definition used by Lovell is modified here to exclude nonaid mandates.

40. Ibid., pp. 35-36.

41. U.S. Office of Management and Budget, *Managing Federal Assistance in the 1980s: Working Papers* (Washington: OMB, August/September, 1979), especially A1-A8.

42. Pub. L. 92-583; and Pub. L. 94-370.

43. Cited in *C.F.R.:* 920.1

44. *C.F.R.* 920.10-920.19.

45. See especially *C.F.R.* 920.14(b) (2) (i).

46. Walter A. Rosenbaum, *The Politics of Environmental Concern,* 2d ed. (New York: Praeger, 1977), p. 219.

47. See Wayne Penn and C. Gregory Buntz, "State Responses to Federal Health Regulatory Requirements," *Journal of Health and Human Resources Administration* 2(3):282-298.

48. Pub. L. 93-641.

49. *Managing Federal Assistance,* p. A-7-7.

50. Ibid., p. A-7-9.

51. Ibid., pp. A-7-9-10.

52. Ibid., pp. A-7-10-11.

53. Ibid., p. A-7-12.

54. The one major possible exception to this was the 1974 amendment to the Fair Labor Standards Act which extended federal minimum wage and maximum hour standards to all state and local employees, but even this is a poor example of horizontal program quality mandates on two grounds: first, although withholding or rescinding federal aid might have been useful as a tool in enforcing these standards, the law itself was a more direct assertion of federal power and could have been implemented through litiga-

tion alone; and second, the amendment was declared unconstitutional in a 1976 decision, National League of Cities v. Usery, 426 U.S. 833.

55. *Managing Federal Assistance,* p. A-6.

56. See ibid., paper A8; also Advisory Commission on Intergovernmental Relations, *Categorical Grants: Their Role and Design,* Report A-52 (Washington: ACIR, 1978).

57. Administrative purposes are those discussed earlier as organizational/procedural and include such requirements as having a single agency dealing with a program area (for example, highways) or requiring that the state supply the granting agency with certain types of program feedback. Political goals are served by using grants in a presidential or other election campaign to draw attention to the incumbent's activities.

58. Often under pressures generated by state and local officials themselves. See Donald H. Haider, *When Governments Come to Washington: Governors, Mayors, and Intergovernmental Lobbying* (New York: Free Press, 1974); also Samuel H. Beer, "The Adoption of General Revenue Sharing: A Case Study in Public Sector Politics," *Public Policy* 24(2): 127-195.

59. Charles H. Levine and Paul L. Posner, "The Centralizing Effects of Austerity on the Intergovernmental System," revision of paper presented at 1979 American Political Science Association meeting, Washington, D.C. Also see the exchange between a resident of a small California city and the city's mayor: Bess Christensen, "Playing the Grants Game in Lompoc," *Business Week,* June 2, 1980, pp. 12 and 15; and letter from E.C. Stevens, "The Other Side of the Coin," *Business Week,* July 7, 1980, p. 4.

60. See David E. Engdahl, "Preemptive Capability of Federal Power," *University of Colorado Law Review* 45(1973):51-88.

61. W. Joseph Heffernan, *Introduction to Social Welfare Policy: Power, Scarcity and Common Human Needs* (Itasca, Ill.: Peacock Publishers, 1979), pp. 134-137.

62. Pub. L. 91-596.

63. Richard Zeckhauser and Albert Nichols, "The Occupational Safety and Health Administration—An Overview," in *Study on Federal Regulation,* Vol. VI: *Framework for Regulation, Appendix* (Washington: Committee on Governmental Affairs, U.S. Senate, 1978), p. 209.

64. Heffernan, *Introduction to Social Welfare Policy,* p. 135.

65. The Surface Mining Control and Reclamation Act of 1977 (Pub. L. 95-87) has the federal government establishing and enforcing strip mining and reclamation standards which can be turned over (in 1981) to those states which demonstrate the ability and willingness to adopt and implement standards at least as stringent. There are certain instances, however, where the preemptory assertion of federal law is vague enough to allow for court interpretations regarding the states' right to adopt and

enforce standards and regulations at least as strict as those set forth by Washington. One such instance is described in Lee S. Weinberg, "Askew v. American Waterways Operators, Inc.: The Emerging New Federalism," *Publius* 8(4):37–53.

66. Pub. L. 91–604.

67. Pub. L. 91–604, sections 108–110.

68. Pub. L. 91–604, section 110(c) (1).

69. Pub. L. 91–604, section 209.

70. Pub. L. 91–604, section 233.

71. Pub. L. 91–604, section 114(b) (1).

72. The Energy Supply and Environmental Coordination Act of 1974 (Pub. L. 93–319) and the Clean Air Act Amendments of 1977 (Pub. L. 95–95).

73. Pub. L. 93–500.

74. Pub. L. 95–619.

75. A number of studies focused on the development and implementation of recent regulatory policies gives credence to this contention. See Charles O. Jones, *Clean Air: The Policies and Politics of Pollution Control* (Pittsburgh: Univ. of Pittsburgh Press, 1975). Also three articles in Charles O. Jones and Robert D. Thomas (eds.), *Public Policy Making in a Federal System*, (Beverly Hills, Calif.: Sage, 1976): Robert D. Thomas, "Intergovernmental Coordination in the Implementation of National Air and Water Pollution Policies," pp. 129–148; Shelton Edner, "Intergovernmental Policy Development: The Importance of Problem Definition" pp. 149–167; and Bruce P. Ball, "Water Pollution and Compliance Decision Making," pp. 169–187.

76. See Mel Dubnick and Alan Gitelson, "Intergovernmental Relations and Regulatory Policy," paper presented at Symposium on Regulatory Policy, November 1979, Houston, Texas.

77. One can read Justice Rehnquist's opinion in *National League of Cities* v. *Usery* to mandate such assistance; see discussion in Laurence H. Tribe, "Unraveling National League of Cities: The New Federalism and Affirmative Rights to Essential Government Services," *Harvard Law Review* 90(6):1091.

78. Christensen, "Playing the Grants Game."

79. See Levine and Posner, "The Centralizing Effects of Austerity."

80. Temporary Commission on City Finances, cited in Levine and Posner, ibid.

81. Christensen, "Playing the Grants Game."

82. John V. Weatherspoon, "Life Among the 'Grunts'," *The Urban Interest* 2(1):52–58.

83. Michael D. Reagan, *The New Federalism* (New York: Oxford Univ. Press, 1972), p. 10.

84. See Dubnick and Gitelson, "Intergovernmental Relations."

85. Rowland and Marz, "Interstate Inequities."

86. The authors would like to thank Eric Anderson, City Manager of Munster, Indiana, for his help in clarifying the political leverage issue.

87. See Aaron Wildavsky's discussion in "A Bias Toward Federalism," in *Speaking Truth to Power: The Art and Craft of Policy Analysis* (Boston: Little, Brown, 1979), chapter 6.

3

Frustrating National Policy: Partial Federal Preemption

Joseph F. Zimmerman

Fundamental changes in intergovernmental relations in the United States have occurred since 1965 as Congress with increasing frequency has exercised its powers of formal preemption and has assumed complete or partial responsibility for many traditional state- and local-government functions.[1] Prior to the 1960s, Congress seldom used its formal authority to preempt state functions. Examples included the Bankruptcy Act of 1933 and the Atomic Energy Act of 1946.[2] Congress, of course, also acquired considerable influence over numerous state-local functions by means of conditional grants-in-aid, and this may be viewed as a type of informal or extraconstitutional partial preemption "voluntarily" initiated by state and local governments accepting federal grants. In addition, Congress dictated the nature of the states' estate tax system and unemployment compensation system by means of tax credits, and this may be categorizied as a second type of informal or extraconstitutional partial preemption.[3]

The decision of the founding fathers to include in the United States Constitution provision for partial and total federal preemption of responsibility for various functions ensured a fluid type of federalism with the actual distribution of formal political powers changing with the passage of time. Nevertheless, it is inconceivable that the founding fathers could have foreseen the extensive growth of federal powers to the point that the federal government today, via informal and formal preemptory actions, significantly determines the scope and nature of state- and local-government services and regulatory activities.

The greatly expanded role of the national government has produced a reallocation of political power between state and local chief executives and their respective legislative bodies and has changed significantly the lobbying activities of private and public interest groups by shifting many of their activities to Washington, D.C. This chapter describes the types of partial congressional preemption and, using the air-pollution problem as an example, draws tentative conclusions about its usefulness as a policymaking instrument.

However, proper understanding of the changing nature of intergovern-

This is a substantially revised version of a paper delivered at the 1979 Annual Meeting of the American Political Science Association, Washington, D.C., September 1, 1979.

mental relations since 1965 first requires a brief review of the intent of the drafters of the United States Constitution in 1787 and the Tenth Amendment in 1789.

The Constitution of 1787

Although the United States Constitution might have been designed to allocate specified functions to each of the two levels of government, a decision was made to delegate enumerated powers only to the national government. Included among those delegated were exclusive powers, such as foreign affairs, coinage of money, post offices, and declaration of war, which states were forbidden to exercise.[4] Alexander Hamilton in *The Federalist Number 32* placed exclusive federal powers in three categories: "where the Constitution in express terms granted an exclusive authority to the Union; where it granted in one instance an authority to the Union, and in another prohibited the States from exercising the like authority; and where it granted an authority to the Union to which a similar authority in the States would be absolutely and totally contradictory and repugnant."[5] The power to establish a uniform rule of naturalization was cited by Hamilton as an example of the third type of exclusive power. The Congress and the states were denied other powers—enacting bills of attainder and ex post facto laws, and granting titles of nobility—by the Constitution.[6]

The Constitution provides for two types of concurrent powers. The first type includes the power to tax, which is not subject to formal preemption.[7] The second type includes powers granted to Congress but not prohibited to the states. In the event of a direct conflict between a federal statute and a state statute, the supremacy clause of the Constitution provides for the prevalence of the federal law by nullifying the state law.[8] In other words, the exercise of this type of concurrent power by a state is subject to complete or partial preemption by Congress. Hamilton in *The Federalist Number 27* wrote that the supremacy clause means that "the legislatures, courts, and magistrates of the respective members [states] will be incorporated into operations of the national government as far as its just and constitutional authority extends, and will be rendered auxiliary to the enforcement of its laws."[9]

The Constitution also contains a list of powers that states may exercise only with the consent of Congress; examples include the levying of import and tonnage duties, keeping of troops in time of peace, and entrance into compacts with other states.[10] The United States Supreme Court, however, has not interpreted these powers to mean that in all cases they may be exercised only with the consent of Congress. The Court held in *Virginia v. Ten-*

nessee (1893) that congressional consent is required only if states desire to enter into "political" compacts, and in 1975, the Court ruled that the prohibition of the levying of "imports or duties on imports" without the consent of Congress does not prohibit the levying of a property tax on imported products. Relative to the latter, the Court wrote:

> Nothing in the history of the Import-Export Clause even remotely suggests that a nondiscriminatory ad valorem property tax which is also imposed on imported goods that are no longer in import transit was the type of extraction that was regarded as objectionable by the Framers of the Constitution. For such an extraction, unlike discriminatory state taxation against imported goods as imports, was not regarded as an impediment that severely hampered commerce or constituted a form of tribute by seaboard States to the disadvantage of the other States.[11]

According to James Madison in *The Federalist Number 45*, "the powers delegated by the proposed Constitution to the federal government are few and defined. Those which are to remain in the State governments are numerous and indefinite."[12] Madison, of course, was referring in particular to the police power. Hamilton in *The Federalist Number 17* assured readers that "it will always be far more easy for the State governments to encroach upon the national authorities than for the national government to encroach upon the State authorities. The proof of this proposition turns upon the greater degree of influence which the State governments, if they administer their affairs with uprightness and prudence, will generally possess over the people. . . ."[13] Madison added, in *The Federalist Number 46,* that "a local spirit will infallibly prevail much more in the members of Congress than a national spirit will prevail in the legislatures of the particular States."[14]

In spite of Publius's assurances that federal powers would be limited under the proposed Constitution, fear of a strong centralized government induced the proponents of the document to agree to the adoption of a Bill of Rights in order to gain sufficient support for ratification of the proposed Constitution. To make crystal clear that the national government possessed only enumerated powers, the Tenth Amendment of the United States Constitution stipulated that "the powers not delegated to the United States by the Constitution, nor prohibited by it to the States, are reserved to the States respectively, or to the people." This division-of-powers approach to government—an *imperium in imperio*—often is labeled *dual* or *layer-cake federalism.* In practice, as is well known, there is a sharing of many powers by the three principal levels of government—federal, state, and local—rather than the complete division of powers suggested by the term *dual federalism.*[15]

Expansion of National Powers

The United States Constitution today in terms of essentials of federal-state relations is a vastly different document than the one that became effective in 1788 because the federal sphere has broadened appreciably through accretion of power resulting from constitutional amendments, statutory elaboration of delegated powers, and judicial interpretation. As a consequence, we find the federal government engaged in activities once considered to be the exlusive responsibilities of state and local governments. This expansion of federal powers has produced a continuing ideological and constitutional debate over the proper roles of the national government and the States.

Constitutional Amendments

No constitutional amendment directly restricted the powers of the states until the Fourteenth Amendment was ratified, with its due process of law, privileges and immunities, and equal protection of the laws clauses. These three clauses have served as the basis for numerous federal court decisions striking down as unconstitutional actions taken by states, including state laws enacted under the reserved police power. The federal courts also have interpreted the due process of law clause to include the First Amendment's guarantees.

The Fifteenth Amendment, adopted in 1870, prohibits the abridgement of the right to vote "because of race, color, or previous condition of servitude" and served as the basis for an 1870 act of Congress enforcing the guarantee and 1871 amendments to the act.[16] In 1875, the United States Supreme Court ruled that the 1870 act was unconstitutional because it was not limited solely to the protection of the voting rights of black citizens since the act also provided for the punishment of those who interfered with the voting right of white citizens.[17] This amendment and the Fourteenth Amendment currently serve as the constitutional basis for the Voting Rights Act of 1965 as amended, which is discussed in greater detail in a subsequent section.

Whereas the Fourteenth Amendment provided the basis for federal judicial intervention in areas that previously had been the responsibility of the states, the Sixteenth Amendment's authorization for Congress to levy a graduated income tax gave the Congress power to raise sufficient funds to finance categorical grant-in-aid programs for state and local governments.[18] With the conditions attached to the grants, Congress and the federal administration have considerable influence over the reserved powers of the states. While states and local governments may avoid the controls inherent in the federal grant-in-aid programs by refusing to apply for and accept grants, the desire to avoid raising state and local taxes and the financial problems of most subnational units make the application for and acceptance of federal grants-in-aid nearly automatic.

The famous Connecticut Compromise leading to the incorporation of the bicameral principle in the United States Constitution involved more than a compromise between the large and small states. The election of United States senators by the legislature of each state was designed to ensure that the interests of each state would be protected in the Congress. Jackson Pemberton, letting the Founding Fathers speak for him, attributes the fundamental changes in federal-state relations to the adoption of the Seventeenth Amendment:

> We noted with concern that the universal nature of legislatures is to legislate too much, and that unless some opposing force were supplied, the United States Congress would eventually infringe every State prerogative until the rights of people vested in the States were consumed. We talked much of the need for Senators to preserve the sovereignty of their States because they were the best defenders of the rights the people had already lost to their States' governments. Hence, Senators were elected by the State legislature, were to answer to the State, and were to represent the interests of the State in the Congress. Amendment 17 destroyed that balance and the Senate became another House.[19]

Statutory Elaboration

Although Congress was delegated specific grants of power in a significant number of important areas of government concern, a few of the delegated powers were not exercised for many decades. To cite only two examples, Congress did not utilize its grant of power to regulate interstate commerce in a comprehensive manner until passage of the Interstate Commerce Act of 1887, nor did it use its supersessive power to regulate bankruptcies until 1933.

However, Congress during the past three and one-half decades increasingly has used its powers of partial and total preemption to supersede state laws. The Atomic Energy Act of 1946, for example, totally preempted responsibility for the regulation of ionizing radiation until a 1959 amendment authorized the former Atomic Energy Commission, now the Nuclear Regulatory Commission, to enter into agreements with states under which a state would be allowed to assume certain regulatory responsibilities.[20] Twenty-five states have done so. Another example of complete supersession is the Uniform Time Act of 1966, which totally preempted responsibility for determining the dates on which standard time is changed to daylight time and vice versa.[21]

As explained in a subsequent section, not all acts approved by Congress and held to be preemptory in nature by the courts contain an explicit preemptory clause. In consequence, it is difficult to determine the precise number of such acts. However, if we limit our discussion to preemptory acts approved since 1965, the number totals approximately seventy.

The most important preemptory actions by Congress involve environmental protection. By the mid-1960s, Congress had decided that a number of areawide problems—particularly environmental ones—could not be eliminated by reliance upon state- and local-government action encouraged by the carrots of federal grants-in-aid. Enactment of two preemptory acts, the Water Quality Act of 1965 and the Air Quality Act of 1967, marked a new phase of partial preemption in congressional exercise of its powers of supersession.[22]

For example, the Water Quality Act required each state to adopt "water quality standards applicable to interstate waters or portions thereof within such State" as well as an implementation and enforcement plan. The administrator of the Environmental Protection Agency (EPA) is authorized to promulgate water-quality standards that become effective at the end of 6 months in the event a state fails to establish adequate standards. The federal role was strengthened by other statutes, particularly the Federal Water Pollution Control Act Amendments of 1972, which established July 1, 1977 as the deadline for the secondary treatment of sewage. The law sets July 1, 1983 as the date for achieving "water quality which provides for protection and propagation of fish, shellfish, and wildlife" and requires the elimination of the "discharge of pollutants into navigable waters by 1985."[23] The Air Quality Act of 1967 established a similar procedure relative to state responsibility for air-pollution abatement with the exception of emissions from new motor vehicles. The implications of these two acts are discussed later.

Judicial Interpretation

As is well known, the U.S. Supreme Court since the development of the doctrine of implied powers in *McCulloch* v. *Maryland* and the doctrine of the continuous journey in *Gibbons* v. *Ogden* has tended to interpret national powers broadly.[24] Relative to implied powers, the Court wrote:

> Among the enumerated powers, we do not find that of establishing a bank or creating a corporation. But there is no phrase in the instrument which, like the Articles of Confederation, excludes incidental or implied powers; and which requires that everything granted shall be expressly and minutely described. Even the Tenth Amendment, which was framed for the purpose of quieting the excessive jealousies which had been excited, omits the

word "expressly," and declares only that the powers "not delegated to the United States, nor prohibited to the States, are reserved to the States or to the people;" thus leaving the question, whether the particular power which may become the subject of contest has been delegated to the one government, or prohibited to the other, to depend on a fair construction of the whole instrument.[25]

Woodrow Wilson in 1885 wrote:

Congress must wantonly go very far outside of the plain and unquestionable meaning of the Constitution, must bump its head directly against all right and precedent, must kick against the very bricks of all well-established rulings and interpretations, before the Supreme Court will offer its distinct rebuke.[26]

Whereas the decisions of the United States Supreme Court limiting the police power of the states relative to economic matters have been well publicized, less public attention has been paid to the recent court decisions extending the First Amendment guarantees by partially preempting state corrupt practices laws that limit political campaign contributions.

State corrupt practices acts since 1976 must conform to the guidelines laid down by the United States Supreme Court in *Buckley* v. *Valeo,* a case involving the Federal Election Campaign Act of 1971 and its amendments of 1974. In this case the Court upheld the individual contribution limits, the disclosure and reporting provisions, and the public-financing provisions, but ruled "that the limitations on campaign expenditures, on independent expenditures by individuals and groups, and on expenditures by a candidate from his personal funds are constitutionally infirm."[27]

The Court specifically held "the Act's expenditure ceilings impose direct and substantial restraints on the quantity of political speech."[28] Relative to the limitations on personal expenditures by candidates, the Court ruled the limitation "imposes a substantial restraint on the ability of persons to engage in protected First Amendment expression."[29] The Court added:

The candidate, no less than any other person, has a First Amendment right to engage in the discussion of public issues and vigorously and tirelessly to advocate his own election and the election of other candidates. Indeed, it is of particular importance that candidates have the unfettered opportunity to make their views known so that the electorate may intelligently evaluate the candidates' personal qualities and their positions on vital public issues before choosing among them on election day.[30]

In 1978, the United States Supreme Court struck down a Massachusetts law restricting corporate contributions to referenda campaigns involving issues "that materially affect its business, property, or assets" by holding that a corporation under the First Amendment to the United States Constitution could spend funds to publicize its views in opposition to a proposed constitutional amendment authorizing the state legislature to levy a graduated income tax.[31]

Federal Preemption

Whereas the expression of fear of the growing power of the federal government reached its zenith with the New Deal in the 1930s, Woodrow Wilson in 1885 wrote about the aggrandizement of power by Congress:

> The plain tendency is toward a centralization of all the greater powers of government in the hands of federal authorities, and toward the practical confirmation of these prerogatives of supreme overlordship which Congress has been gradually appropriating to itself. The central government is constantly becoming stronger and more active, and Congress is establishing itself as the one sovereign authority in that government.[32]

Writing in 1959, Felix Morley offered an explanation for the drift of power to Washington:

> State governments, with a few honorable exceptions, are both ill-designed and ill-equipped to cope with the problems which a dynamic society cannot, or will not, solve for itself. State Constitutions are in many cases unduly restrictive. Their legislatures meet too briefly and have the most meager technical assistance. . . . Governors generally have inadequate executive control over a pattern of local government unnecessarily complex and confusing.[33]

An English observer of the American federal system, Professor D.W. Brogan, concluded in 1960 that states possessed relatively few important powers:

> Of the division of powers, probably the least important today is that between the Union and the States. There is, of course, an irreducible minimum of federalism. The States can never be reduced to being mere counties, but in practice, they may be little more than mere counties. The Union may neglect to exercise powers that it has and so leave them to the States (subject to varying Supreme Court doctrines as to whether the States can legislate freely in the mere absence of federal legislation, on matters affecting interstate commerce for instance). But in a great many fields of modern legislation, states' rights are a fiction, because the economic and social integration of the United States has gone too far for them to remain a reality. They are, in fact, usually argued for, not by zealots believing that the States can do better than the Union in certain fields, but by prudent calculators who know that the States can do little or nothing, which is what the defenders of states' rights want them to do.[34]

Professor Brogan's view of the American federal system in 1960 was an overstatement of the role of the federal government and an understatement of the role of the states. Until the 1960s, the exercise of formal preemptory powers by Congress did not affect intergovernmental relations greatly. Support for this conclusion is based in part on a comparison of the January 1940 issue of *The Annals,* which was devoted to "Intergovernmental Relations in the United States" and contains no reference to formal federal preemption, with a similar volume of *The Annals,* published in 1974, which contains several references to the latter.[35]

Prior to 1960, however, the national government acquired significant influence over many state-local activities by means of the informal partial preemption initiated by conditional federal grants-in-aid and the use of tax credits by Congress.

Informal Preemption

The Hatch Act of 1887, designed to promote agricultural research, was the first federal law authorizing grants-in-aid to the states on a continuing basis. Seven years later, Congress enacted the Carey Act, which contained the first condition, a type of de facto partial preemption, for the receipt of federal funds by states, that is, preparation of a comprehensive plan for the irrigation of arid land. Federal inspection of state operations and matching requirements date from 1911.[36] According to the United States Advisory Commission on Intergovernmental Relations, the use of conditional grants-in-aid by the federal government has been encouraged by the United States Constitution since grants avoid "the legal issues that would be involved in the direct national provision of many domestic services. Because grants operate primarily through state and local governments and because participation is voluntary, not mandatory, they have been subject less to challenge on constitutional grounds."[37]

In dollar amounts, federal grants to state and local governments increased from $7 million in 1902 to $12 million in 1913 to $232 million in 1932 to $1,031 million in 1939.[38] The impact of the sharp increase in federal grants upon state governments did not elude the scrutiny of perceptive observers. Writing in 1940, G. Homer Durham pointed out that "some of the largest and politically most powerful state agencies, such as highway administration with an almost total absence of merit personnel, are no longer dependent on their operating jurisdictions for funds."[39]

The dollar amounts of federal grants-in-aid to state and local governments exploded after World War II and reached a total of $6,838 million in 1960 and $8,324 million in 1963.[40] The United States Advisory Commission on Intergovernmental Relations in 1978 wrote that "at least through the 1950s, federal assistance activities were confined by an effort to restrict aid to fields clearly involving the national interest or an important national purpose."[41] Commencing with 1965, however, "the concept of the national interest lost most of its substantive content" with "any action passed by both legislative chambers and signed by the President being accepted as appropriate."[42]

Addressing the National Governors' Conference on February 24, 1976, Vice-President Nelson A. Rockefeller traced the flow of power toward the national government:

> Consequently, the respective Congress and Administrations, particularly after the steep federal income tax increases during World War II, became the focal points of pressure for meeting all kinds of demands.
>
> These ranged all the way from health and welfare to house paint components to environmental clean-ups. The more detailed the legislation and the more new functions that were added, the more the demands increased.
>
> Federal action and federal money became the goal of pressure groups and politicians alike. Federal funds appeared to be inexhaustible and federal power to achieve desired social change looked limitless.[43]

Extensive informal preemption by the federal government by means of conditional grants-in-aid in recent years has led to fears that state and local governments are becoming stipendiaries and ministerial arms of the federal government, depending heavily on it for funding and no longer possessing discretion to modify federally aided programs because the rulemaking power resides in federal administrative agencies or to reduce funds for federally aided programs because of maintenance-of-effort provisions.

States also have lost the power to reorganize state agencies administering federally aided programs because of the federal single-agency requirement, a requirement recently upheld by the United States Supreme Court.[44] Charles L. Schultze questions whether major national purposes are served by conditional grants-in-aid and maintains that the grants "simply reflect the substitution of the judgment of federal legislators and agency officials for that of state and local officials."[45]

Recognition also must be afforded to the veto power of federal administrators over state plans, policies, and program implementation. In other words, there has been a significant expansion of the decision-making powers of federal administrators, and the expansion has evoked fears of administrative imperialism. Former United States Senator James L. Buckley in 1978 expressed this viewpoint in strong terms:

> The federal bureaucracy has grown into what is essentially a fourth branch of government that has become virtually immune to political direction or control. It is peopled by men and women who are now possessed of broad discretionary power over many areas of American life—so many, in fact,

that one begins to wonder to what extent ours can still be described as a government of laws rather than of men.[46]

In Buckley's view, the federal machinery has been overloaded. He is convinced that only by shifting responsibilities to the states and local governments will it be possible to reduce federal involvement in the governance process and to "expand the amount of time that the President and the members of Congress can devote to each of the matters for which they remain responsible."[47]

Although the rhetoric of some state officials suggests that states are becoming vassals of the federal government, this description is an inaccurate portrayal of the powers of states because they continue to be important units of government possessing relatively broad discretionary powers in areas such as land use, public health, and police and fire protection. Furthermore, states retain a considerable amount of discretionary authority in administering federally aided programs; they also are able to influence federal policies contained in statutes enacted by Congress and in rules and regulations promulgated by federal agencies administering the grant programs.

State Appropriation of Federal Funds

Federal grants-in-aid have strengthened the position of the governor vis-à-vis the legislature in the typical state, since most federal grants are for and received by executive agencies under the control of the governor. A survey of state budget officers by the United States Advisory Commission on Intergovernmental Relations revealed that federal grants requiring no state matching or only in-kind matching "strengthens the discretionary power of the Governor and administrators and weakens the Legislature's control over the budget and administration."[48] In consequence, the governor is less dependent on appropriations by the legislature than he would be in the absence of federal grants. This is the reason that a controversy has raged over the question of whether all federal funds received by the state should be placed in the general fund of the state treasury and be subject to appropriation by the legislature.

In New York State, for example, the legislature feared that federal grants would allow departments and agencies to engage in activities opposed by the legislature. To obtain information on federal grants activity, the 1966 legislature enacted a law forbidding state departments and agencies to apply for federal funds unless the director of the budget and the chairmen of the fiscal committees of the legislature are notified in writing 30 days in advance of an application.[49] This law has not proved satisfactory to the legislature, and the leaders of the two houses in 1978 introduced a bill that declared "that comprehensive allocation and planning of state expenditures from all funding sources is necessary to assure that limited state resources are used to their maximum potential."[50]

The New York Legislature was disturbed by the fact that it had directed the State Education Department in 1976 to abolish several administrative positions and associated support personnel, but discovered that at least seven of the positions were continued with federal funds.[51] The year previously, for instance, the legislature reduced the $600,000 request of the department for the instructional support system to $300,000 and later discovered the department had used $350,000 in federal funds to supplement the state appropriation.

Questions have been raised as to the constitutionality of the proposed New York law; for example, courts in Colorado and New Mexico have ruled that federal funds are "custodial funds" controlled exclusively by the executive branch and are not subject to legislative reappropriation.[52] However, in 1973, the U.S. Supreme Court ruled that a state may reappropriate federal funds provided federal requirements are complied with.[53] And in 1979, the Court upheld a ruling of the Pennsylvania Supreme Court regarding the constitutionality of a requirement that all federal funds be deposited in the general fund of the state and be available for appropriation by the legislature.[54]

Federal funds have not always strengthened the position of the governor. An extreme example of administrative disintegration caused by federal funds occurred in Massachusetts in the late 1950s and early 1960s when four private corporations were established by state agencies for the receipt of federal grants. The Massachusetts Commissioner of Public Health, for example, applied for federal grants and directed that the grants be sent to the Massachusetts Health Research Institute, Inc. The Institute was a private corporation headed by the Commissioner and administered primarily by employees of the Department of Public Health. The corporate arrangement allowed the department to evade the state's personnel, salary, and other controls over the spending of public funds.

Formal Preemption

Many federal laws contain an express provision for total federal preemption. The Flammable Fabrics Act stipulates that "this Act is intended to supersede any law of any State or political subdivision thereof inconsistent with its provisions."[55] Similarly, the United States Grain Standards Act forbids states or political subdivisions to "require the inspection or description in accordance with any standards of kind, class, quality, condition, or other characteristics of grain as a condition of shipment, or sale of such grain in interstate or foreign commerce, or require license for, or impose any other restrictions upon, the performance of any official inspection function under this Act by official inspection personnel." The Radiation Control for Health and Safety Act of 1968 forbids state and local governments "to establish . . . any standard which is applicable to the same aspect of the performance of such product and which is not identical to the federal standard."[57]

Another type of total federal preemption is illustrated by the Gun Control Act of 1968: "No provision of this chapter shall be construed as indicating an intent on the part of the Congress to occupy the field in which such provision operates to the exclusion of the law of any State on the same subject matter, unless there is a direct and positive conflict between such provision and the law of the State so that the two cannot be reconciled or consistently stand together."[58] A similar provision is contained in the Drug Abuse Control Amendment of 1965.[59]

The Federal Railroad Safety Act of 1970 specifically authorizes states to adopt laws, rules, regulations, orders, and standards relating to railroad safety that are more stringent than the counterpart federal ones "when necessary to eliminate or reduce an essentially local safety hazard, and when not incompatible with any federal law, rule, regulation, order, or standard, and when not creating an undue burden on interstate commerce."[60]

Partial federal preemption statutes establish minimum national standards and authorize states to continue to be responsible for regulatory activity provided the state standards are at least as high as the national standards. The Safe Drinking Water Act, for example, stipulates that "a State has primary enforcement responsibility for public water systems" provided the administrator of the Environmental Protection Agency determines that the state "has adopted drinking water regulations which . . . are no less stringent than" national standards.[61] Should a state fail to adopt or enforce such standards, the EPA would apply national standards within that state.

A second type of partial federal preemption is illustrated by the Wholesome Meat Act, which grants the Secretary of Agriculture the authority to inspect meat and transfer responsibility for meat inspection to a state that has enacted a law requiring meat inspection and reinspection consistent with federal standards.[62] This act also allows states to transfer responsibility for inspection of meat for intrastate commerce to the United States Department of Agriculture. To date, eighteen states have initiated such a transfer. The Poultry Products Inspection Act contains provisions similar to the Wholesome Meat Act, and a total of twenty-six states have transferred responsibility for inspecting poultry products to the United States Department of Agriculture.[63] A third example of partial federal preemption is the Occupational Safety and Health Act of 1970, which encourages states to assume responsibility for the development and enforcement of safety and health standards meeting federal standards by submitting a state plan to the Secretary of Labor for approval.[64] This act differs from the Wholesome Meat Act and the Poultry Products Inspection Act by containing a section stipulating that "nothing in this Act shall prevent any state agency or court from asserting jurisdiction under state law over any occupational safety or health issue with respect to which no [federal] standard is in effect."

Many acts of Congress do not contain an explicit partial or total preemption section, yet have been held by courts to be preemptive. In 1941, the U.S. Supreme Court stressed that each challenge of a state law on the ground of inconsistency with federal law must be determined on the basis of the particular facts of the case:

> There is not—and from the very nature of the problem—there cannot be any rigid formula or rule which can be used to determine the meaning and purpose of every act of Congress. This Court, in considering the validity of state laws in the light of treaties or federal laws touching on the same subject, has made use of the following expressions: conflicting; contrary to; occupying the field; repugnance; difference; irreconcilability; inconsistency; violation; curtailment; and interference. But none of these expressions provides an infallible constitutional test or an exclusive constitutional yardstick. In the final analysis, there can be no one crystal clear distinctly marked formula. Our primary function is to determine whether, under the circumstances of this particular case, Pennsylvania's law stands as an obstacle to the accomplishment and execution of the full purposes and objections of Congress.[65]

In 1947, the United States Supreme Court explicated two tests of federal preemption: (1) "the question in each case is what the purpose of Congress was," and (2) does the act of Congress involve "a field in which the federal interest is so dominant that the federal system will be assumed to preclude enforcement of state laws on the same subject?"[66] For example, the Court wrote relative to the Noise Control Act of 1972:

> Our prior cases on preemption are not precise guidelines in the present controversy, for each case turns on the peculiarities and special features of the federal regulatory scheme in question. . . . Control of noise is of course deep-seated in the police power of the States. Yet the pervasive control vested in EPA [Environmental Protection Agency] and FAA [Federal Aviation Administration] under the 1972 Act seems to us to leave not room for local curfews or other local controls.[67]

The U.S. Supreme Court has placed some limits on federal preemptory powers. Congress in 1970 lowered the voting age in all elections to eighteen, but the Court ruled that Congress lacked the power to lower the voting age for state and local elections.[68] Justice Hugo L. Black, in delivering the judg-

ment of the Court, wrote that "the Equal Protection Clause of the Fourteenth Amendment was never intended to destroy the States' power to
govern themselves, making the Nineteenth and Twenty-fourth Amendments
superfluous."[69] Justice Black added that the power of Congress to enforce
the guarantees of Fourteenth and Fifteenth Amendments was subject to at
least three limitations:

> First, Congress may not by legislation repeal other provisions of the Con-
> stitution. Second, the power granted to Congress was not intended to strip
> the States of their power to govern themselves or to convert our national
> government of enumerated powers into a central government of unre-
> strained authority over every inch of the whole Nation. Third, Congress
> may only "enforce" the provisions of the amendments and may do so only
> by "appropriate legislation."[70]

In 1976, the Court invalidated the 1974 Fair Labor Standards Act
Amendments, extending minimum-wage and overtime-pay provisions to
nonsupervisory employees of state and local governments on the ground the
extension violated the Tenth Amendment to the United States Constitution
and threatened the "separate and independent existence" of the units.[71] The
same year, the Court held that a written examination for applications for a
police department was not unconstitutional simply because a "substantially
disproportionate" burden is placed on blacks.[72] The following year, this
decision was applied to housing and school desegregation cases with the
result that school and housing desegregation can be ordered by United
States District Courts on a metropolitanwide basis only if there is direct
evidence that actions were taken deliberately by suburban governments to
prevent housing and school integration in the past.[73] In 1979, moreover,
the Court ruled that the statute giving federal courts jurisdiction over allega-
tions of violations of constitutional rights does not cover a suit based simply
on the fact that a state law conflicts with the federal Social Security Act.[74]
Conceding that the conflict between the laws violates the supremacy clause
of the United States Constitution, the Court held that such a violation is not
the type of constitutional allegation that confers jurisdiction on federal
courts.

However, these cases have been the exceptions rather than the rule. The
major reasons for the sharp increase in federal preemptory action since 1965
are the growing recognition of the interstate nature of many public problems, the general failure of states to launch effective corrective programs
to solve the problems, the establishment of environmental and public-inter-
est groups that have lobbied effectively in Washington, and concomitant
public support for federal-governmental action to solve environmental
problems in particular.

States on occasion have attempted to forestall federal preemptive
action by promoting the adoption of uniform state laws and entering into

interstate compacts creating agencies with the power to solve problems. Successful efforts of this nature include the Atlantic States Marine Fisheries Commission and the Interstate Oil Compact. An unsuccessful example is the Mid-Atlantic States Air Pollution Control Compact entered into by Connecticut, New Jersey, and New York subsequent to President Johnson's message to Congress recommending federal preemption of responsibility for air-pollution abatement.[75] Congress did not grant its consent to the proposed compact.

Commencing in 1971, questions began to be raised about federal preemption and fears began to be expressed about the potential danger of an incipient monocentric system of government. Who in 1788 would have believed that a bill approved by the state legislature and signed by the governor, other than a bill falling within the purview of section 10 of Article I of the United States Constitution, would require the approval of the United States Attorney General or the United States District Court for the District of Columbia before the law could be implemented? Yet the federal Voting Rights Act contains such a requirement for states and their political subdivisions which meet the two criteria for triggering the act.[76]

Dissenting in *Perkins* v. *Matthews,* a voting rights case, Justice Hugo L. Black wrote:

> In my view, the Constitution prohibits the Federal Government from requiring federal approval of state laws before they can become effective. Proposals for such congressional veto power over state laws were made at the Constitutional Convention and overwhelmingly rejected. The Fourteenth Amendment did not alter the basic structure of our federal system of government. The Fourteenth Amendment did bar discrimination on account of race and did give the Federal Government power to enforce the ban on racial discrimination. In this case the Congress has attempted to enforce the ban on racial discrimination by requiring States to submit their laws or practices to federal approval even before they are initiated. In my view that requirement attempts to accomplish the constitutional end of banning racial discrimination by a means—requiring submission of proposed state laws to the Attorney General—that violates the letter and spirit of the Constitution.[77]

Brevard Crihfield and H. Clyde Reeves of the Council of State Governments in 1974, while not maintaining that all preemptive actions by Congress are wrong, were highly critical of indiscriminate supersession of state laws by Congress:

> Regulation of everybody and everything is not necessarily the *Summum Bonum* of a legislative assembly, be it state or national. Legislative forbearance, like judicial restraint, has its place in the body politic. Congress is often urged to supersede state law as a means of promoting uniform applications throughout the nation, and on occasion the need will be

manifest. On the other hand, interstate cooperative devices have shown their ability to achieve necessary uniformity and coordination in many areas of public concern. A federal system of government, by definition, envisions finer intergovernmental tuning devices than a centric doctrine.[78]

Preemptive decisions of the United States Supreme Court since 1954 have led to the filing of numerous congressional bills limiting the Court's jurisdiction as authorized by the United States Constitution.[79] To cite only one recent example, in 1979, Senator Jesse A. Helms of North Carolina introduced a bill—S. 438—stipulating that "the Supreme Court shall not have jurisdiction to review, by appeal, writ of certiorari, or otherwise, any case arising out of any state statute, ordinance, rule, regulation, or any part thereof, or arising out of any Act interpreting, applying, or enforcing a state statute, ordinance, rule, or regulation, which relates to voluntary prayers in public schools and public buildings."[80] The bill, which also denies jurisdiction over such cases to United States District Courts, was approved by the Senate on April 5, 1979 by a vote of forty-seven to thirty-seven.[81]

New Role for the Governor. Federal preemptive laws, rules, and regulations delegate powers to governors of states that are not established in their state constitutions and statutes. In other words, partial federal preemption changes the balance of power between the governor and the state legislature and has the greatest impact on states where the governor has limited formal powers.

An examination of ten major federal preemptive acts and one federal executive order reveals that the governor has been granted new powers, including several of great potential importance. These grants of powers may be placed in eleven general categories.

The first type of power is *specific authorization* in the preemption statute for the governor to submit a plan to a federal agency. The federal Environmental Pesticide Control Act of 1972 stipulates that if a state desires to assume responsibility for certification of pesticides applicators, the governor must submit a plan to the administrator of the Environmental Protection Agency for approval.[82] A related provision is found in the Clean Air Act Amendment of 1977, which requires that the Administrator of EPA who is required to review state implementation plans within 18 months of the submission, consult the governor before requiring a revision of the plans.[83]

The second category involves the *annual certification* of state plans. The Federal Water Pollution Control Act Amendments of 1972 stipulate that the governor or his designee annually shall certify areawide waste-treatment management plans.[84]

The *certification of state compliance* with a national requirement is a third category of powers granted to governors. The Emergency Highway Energy Conservation Act of 1974 established a national speed limit of 55 mph, and the Federal Highway Administration issued implementing regulations stipulating that "each Governor shall submit to the Federal Highway Administrator . . . a statement that the State" is complying with the speed limit.[85]

Authority to issue *temporary permits* is a fourth category of powers granted to governors. The Safe Drinking Water Act of 1974 empowers the administrator of the Environmental Protection Agency, upon application of the governor of a state, to issue "one or more temporary permits each of which is applicable to a particular injection well and to the underground injection of a particular fluid. . . ."[86]

A fifth category of powers delegated to governors by federal preemption statutes is authority to request the *waiver of the single-agency requirement.* The Federal Metal and Nonmetallic Mine Safety Act of 1966 authorizes the Secretary of Labor, "upon request of the Governor . . . , to waive the single State agency provision hereof and approve another State administrative structure or arrangement if the Secretary determines that the objectives of this Act will not be endangered by the use of such other State structure or arrangement."[87]

Authority to *request that the state assume responsibility* for a federally preempted function is a sixth category of powers granted to governors by federal preemption statutes. Such authority is contained in the Wholesome Meat Act of 1967 and the Poultry Products Inspection Act of 1968.[88]

A category of power that is of more importance than the preceding is the *designation of a state agency* to be responsible for the preempted function. The National Health Planning and Resources Development Act of 1974 authorizes the governor of a state to designate a state agency as the State Health Planning and Development Agency.[89] The Federal Water Pollution Control Act Amendments of 1972 contain two provisions authorizing the governor to identify areas with "substantial water quality control problems," define the boundaries of each area, and designate "a single representative organization, including elected officials from local governments or their designees, capable of developing effective areawide waste treatment management plans for such areas," and designate "one or more waste treatment management agencies . . . for each area. . . ."[90] These are referred to as *section 208 agencies.* The Clean Air Act Amendments of 1977 contain a similar provision authorizing "the Governor (or, in the case of an interstate area, Governors), after consultation with elected officials of local governments in the affected area, or a State agency to prepare such plan."[91] The Federal Environmental Pesticide Control Act of 1972 also authorizes the governor to designate a state agency to be responsible for the certification of applicators of pesticides.[92] In addition, many conditional grant-in-aid programs authorize the governor to designate a state agency. The Surface Transportation Assistance Act of 1978, for instance, authorizes the governor to designate metropolitan planning organizations.[93]

The eighth category of powers granted to the governor by act of Congress is the *authority to appoint members* of a state council. The National Health Planning and Resources Development Act of 1974 provides that the Statewide Health Coordinating Council be appointed by the governor.[94]

A ninth category of power granted to the governor by federal preemption statutes is responsibility for *administration of programs* and is illustrated by the following provision found in the Highway Safety Act of 1966: "The Secretary [of Transportation] shall not approve any State highway safety program under this section which does not (A) provide that the Governor of the State shall be responsible for the administration of the program."[95] This provision, of course, means that the legislature cannot decide to place responsibility for state highway safety programs in an agency independent of the governor. In 1973, Governor Nelson A. Rockefeller of New York, for example, established by executive order an Interdepartmental Traffic Safety Committee as the state agency in charge of state highway-safety programs.[96]

A tenth category is exemplified by the establishment of an allocation system during a period of gasoline shortages in which power is *delegated by the president* to the governor.[97] This is in contrast to the usual delegation authorization incorporated in legislation.

The eleventh and potentially most important category is the grant of powers to the governor by the Clean Air Act Amendments to *redesignate areas* with certain specified exceptions from Class I, where new pollution is not allowed, to Class III, where deterioration up to secondary standards is allowed.[98] In effect, the redesignation provision allows the governor to arbitrate the balance between economic development and preservation of air quality, provided pollutants emanating from new development do not exceed national standards.

Federal Preemption and Goal Achievement: A Case Study

A major reason for federal preemptive action since 1965 has been the belief of Congress that conditional grants-in-aid have failed to induce adequate state- and local-government action to solve many major public problems.[99] Even with the assistance of federal grants, state and local governments often were slow to develop plans for corrective action and even slower to implement the plans in many instances. A second major reason for initiation of preemptive action by Congress was the growing recognition of the interstate nature of many problems, environmental ones in particular, and the need for uniform corrective action on a national basis. With a few exceptions, Congress did not preempt total responsibility because of the diversity of conditions in a large nation and the limited capacity of the federal executive branch to assume complete responsibility for the preempted functions. Sufficient time has elapsed since 1965 to permit tentative conclusions about the success of partial federal preemption relative to the use of conditional grants-in-aid in attaining national goals such as air quality. From the case study one can sense the enormous complexity of, and conflict in, political relationships brought into play by partial rather than total preemption.

The Clean Air Amendments of 1970 represented a sharp break with the earlier federal air-pollution-abatement efforts which relied on the leadership of state and local government and took into consideration the economic and technical feasibility of abatement controls. In the 1970 amendments, direct federal action to protect public health was made national policy and explicit dates for adoption of standards and abatement plans by states were established.[100]

The administrator of the Environmental Protection Agency was directed to publish within 90 days the categories of stationary sources of air pollution subject to performance standards established under the amendments. Each state was authorized to submit proposed procedures for implementing and enforcing standards of performance for new sources and the EPA Administrator was empowered to authorize each state to implement and enforce the standards for other than new U.S.-owned sources. On February 24, 1974, the administrator published final regulations for reviewing the air-quality impact prior to construction of new facilities—labeled *indirect sources*—that might generate significant amounts of automobile traffic.[101]

If stationary-source controls, combined with motor-vehicle emission controls, cannot ensure the attainment of statutory ambient air-quality standards within an air-quality control region, transportation controls must be adopted. Such controls can force significant changes on residents of the region. In April 1973, Governor Nelson A. Rockefeller and Mayor John V. Lindsay transmitted an air-quality implementation plan for the New York City metropolitan area to the administrator of the Environmental Protection Agency.[102] The plan, approved by EPA in June 1973, provided for the imposition of transportation controls, including mandatory vehicle emission inspection, tolling of East River and Harlem River bridges in New York City, staggering of work hours, a sharp reduction in the number of midtown Manhattan parking spaces, improved traffic management, designation of exclusive bus lanes, and a selective ban on taxicab cruising in midtown Manhattan. In 1974, the United States Second Circuit Court of

Appeals upheld the validity of the plan.[103] Following his election to office, however, Mayor Abraham Beame, in 1975, sought to amend the New York City metropolitan area transportation control plan to eliminate the requirement for tolling of the bridges and vehicle emission inspection.

Although the mayor was unsuccessful in his attempt to amend the plan, he and other officials were able to convince the New York State congressional delegation to work for the inclusion of a provision in the Clean Air Act Amendments of 1977 directing the EPA Administrator to delete a requirement for the tolling of bridges upon application of the governor of the concerned state. The provision was subsequently incorporated into the act.[104] In October 1977, Governor Hugh L. Carey applied to EPA for removal of the tolling provision, and the requirement was deleted from the plan in November.[105] However, even then the city-state-federal problem involving the plan was not resolved completely.

In November 1976, the EPA brought suit against the state to force the implementation of the vehicle emissions testing program. In June 1977, United States District Court Judge Kevin Duffy declared the state to be in violation of the emission-control requirement and directed the state to initiate an annual emission inspection system for all motor vehicles registered in the city and Nassau, Suffolk, Westchester, and Rockland Counties by September 1, 1979. The situation was further complicated by the 1977 Clean Air Act requirement that a state submit a revised transportation-implementation plan by July 1, 1979 in order to attain national primary ambient air-quality standards by December 31, 1972.[106] The amendments also authorized a delay until December 31, 1987 in the achievement of the standards if a state demonstrated to EPA that it had severe oxidants and carbon monoxide problems making the attainment of the federal standards by December 31, 1982 impossible.[107]

Although Governor Carey requested the legislature to mandate a motor vehicle emission inspection system for the New York City metropolitan area and to appropriate the necessary funds, the State Senate as of early June 1980 refused to accede to the request, arguing that the best approach would be a pilot implementation program and that the federal government should help to fund it. In the meantime, the governor, in late 1979, announced that the Commissioner of Motor Vehicles possessed sufficient authority to order an emission inspection program to be financed by a fee.[108] (This inspection, it must be pointed out, is a very limited one and would not achieve the goals outlined in the 1973 air quality implementation plan for the New York City metropolitan area.)

Referring to the complexity created by the Clean Air Amendments of 1970, Representative Barry Goldwater Jr. of California, in 1979, stated "we are wallowing in bureaucratic haze as thick as the smog in Los Angeles on a hot summer day. . . . I have come to the conclusion that our messy concoction of regulations, procedures, guidelines, and mandates are creating more aggravation than they are worth." [sic][109] Representative Goldwater also stressed that the failure of the majority of air-quality controls regions to meet ambient air-quality standards as late as 1 year after the original deadline should have led to questioning of the approach and added:

> The 1977 amendments . . . have revised the timetable again, but in talking with officials at the Environmental Protection Agency, and with agency heads in California at the state and local level, I am convinced that this standard of procrastination has become par for the course. Let us face it— we are bogged down in a cesspool of government rules which have already impacted on our economic growth and program to achieve energy self-sufficiency at a time when the economy and our energy situation are both very uncertain. [110]

The lessening of air-pollution standards also has resulted in inter-regional friction. Acid rain, which is produced from sulfur and nitrogen emitted by Midwest power plants and factories, has killed marine life in lakes in the Adirondack Mountains of New York and has produced pressure by New York and other northeastern states to force the EPA to reduce the emission of such pollutants in the Midwest.[111] The EPA also relaxed pollution standards for individual power plants, such as two operated by Cleveland Electric Illuminating Company which produce more air pollution than all Consolidated Edison Company power plants in New York State.[112]

The 1977 amendments also directed each state to submit a revised state implementation plan to EPA by December 1, 1978, and the agency was to approve acceptable revised plans by June 30, 1979. If a state did not have an approved plan by that date, the state could not grant permits for the construction of new industrial facilities in areas not attaining ambient air-quality standards.[113]

By the June deadline, no state had its plan approved, and twenty-two states and territories had not submitted revised plans to the agency. By April 21, 1980, all states and one territory submitted partial or complete plans, and notice of proposed rulemaking had been published in the *Federal Register* for forty-eight states. In addition, final action had been taken by the agency on complete nonattainment plans for fifteen states and for portions of plans of fifteen other states.

An examination of submitted plans reveals that many were inadequate and would not result in the achievement of the ambient air quality mandated by the Clean Air Act Amendments of 1977. A number of plans submitted by states called for an extension of the attainment dates for the carbon monoxide and ozone standards from December 31, 1982 to December 31, 1987.[114] Achievement of the standards by the latter date is doubtful and dependent on actions of questionable effectiveness, such as motor vehicle emission inspections.

The failure of partial federal preemption to achieve air-quality standards was highlighted in the Tenth Annual Report of the Council on Environmental Quality:

> In 1977, the air in 2 of 41 urban areas for which reliable data were available still registered in the "unhealthful" range for more than two-thirds of the days of the year. These two, the New York and Los Angeles urban areas, together contain almost 8 percent of the nation's population. Only 16 of the 41 urban areas had "unhealthful readings for fewer than 10 percent of the days during the year." In 3 cities, air pollution appears to have gotten worse between 1974 and 1977. The pollutants that most frequently drove index readings into the "unhealthful" range in the 41 urban areas were carbon monoxide and photochemical oxidants [ozone].[115]

Summary and Conclusions

This chapter has reviewed the writings of Alexander Hamilton and James Madison relative to the distribution of political power between the national government and the states; traced briefly the expansion of national powers through constitutional amendments, statutory elaboration, and judicial interpretation; examined the limitations on national powers; classified federal preemption as informal and formal, with the latter divided into total and partial preemption; analyzed briefly the impact of informal federal preemption on the powers of the governor and the state legislature; described the powers granted to the governor by federal partial preemption statutes and administrative rules and regulations; and discussed federal preemption and goal achievement relative to air quality.

One can conclude without fear of contradiction that states have been deprived of the exclusive sphere of governmental authority intended by the framers of the Tenth Amendment to the United States Constitution. However, in spite of the rhetoric of some state and local officials, there is no evidence that the substantial expansion of federal power through informal and formal preemption has resulted in the atrophy of state and local governments.

The reader should note that not all state and local officials oppose federal preemption. Experience with federal partial preemption reveals that states initiated socially desirable programs privately favored by some state legislators and administrators that probably would not have been implemented in the absence of federal preemption because the programs were too explosive politically on the state level. An analogy can be drawn with local government elected officials who privately support certain state mandates on local governments because it may not be politically possible for a local government to initiate a program in the absence of a state directive.[116]

Available evidence suggests that various interest groups will continue to pressure Congress to exercise its powers of preemption and that in exercising these powers in the future Congress will continue to place reliance on partial federal preemption. Other interest groups will continue to pressure Congress to lessen the federal standards and will be most successful in the environmental area. The energy shortage and the public's reaction to long gasoline lines undoubtedly will persuade members of Congress, especially representatives who must stand for reelection every 2 years, to relax the air-quality standards. The public's reaction to inflation also will benefit interest groups seeking reduced water-quality standards.

The relationship between the levels of government has become so complex and intertwined under partial federal preemption that the average citizen is unable to comprehend the system or to determine who is responsible for failure to achieve goals. The lack of citizen understanding of the existing system and the failure of the system to achieve congressionally mandated goals suggest that consideration should be given to the relative advantages of alternative methods of achieving national goals.

This chapter has discussed three alternative methods of achieving national goals—informal federal preemption by means of conditional grants-in-aid and tax credits that rely on fiscal pressure for compliance, total federal preemption involving direct federal administration of programs, and partial federal preemption with state standards either the same as or higher than federal standards. In addition, consideration can be given to placing greater reliance on contractual federal-state partnerships in the form of federal-state compacts, such as the Appalachian Regional Compact and the Delaware River Basin Compact. The federal government also can place heavier reliance on conditional loans to public and private organizations, contracts with private firms for the performance of functions, increased technical assistance to state and local governments, and an expanded revenue-sharing program.

In deciding on the best method for achieving national goals, consideration must be given to equity in the financing and provision of services, effectiveness of regulations and service provision, economy and efficiency in regulatory activities and service provision, and responsiveness to the citizenry.

Notes

1. *Formal preemption* refers to the authority granted to the Congress by the United States Constitution to assume partial or total responsibility for a governmental function.

2. Bankruptcy Act of 1933, 47 Stat. 1467, 11 U.S.C. 101 (1933); Atomic Energy Act of 1946, 60 Stat. 755, 42 U.S.C. 2011 (1946).

3. Revenue Act of 1926, 44 Stat. 9, 48 U.S.C. 845 (1926); and Social Security Act of 1935, 49 Stat. 620, 42 U.S.C. 301 (1935). These acts forced states to adopt uniform inheritance, estate, and unemployment compensation taxes to prevent the loss of revenue to the national government since the acts allow credits to be deducted by affected taxpayers from their federal tax liabilities for similar taxes paid to states.

4. United States Constitution, Art. I, secs. 8 and 10.

5. *The Federalist Papers* (New York: New American Library, 1961), p. 198.

6. United States Constitution, Art. I, secs. 9 and 10.

7. Ibid., sec. 8.

8. Ibid., Art. VI, sec. 2.

9. *The Federalist Papers,* p. 177.

10. United States Constitution, Art. I, sec. 10.

11. Michelin Tire Corporation v. Wages, 423 U.S. 276 (1975), at 286.

12. *The Federalist Papers,* p. 292.

13. Ibid., p. 119.

14. Ibid., p. 296.

15. For the historical development of cooperative federalism, see Daniel J. Elazar, *American Federalism: A View from the States,* 2d ed. (New York: Crowell, 1972); and Morton Grodzins, *The American System* (Chicago: Rand McNally, 1967). The latter work was edited by Daniel J. Elazar after the death of Professor Grodzins. See also Edward S. Corwin, *National Supremacy* (New York: Holt, 1913); and Edward S. Corwin, *The Commerce Power versus States' Rights* (Princeton: Princeton Univ. Press, 1936).

16. 16 Stat. 140 (1870); and 16 Stat. 433 (1871).

17. United States v. Reese, 92 U.S. 214 (1875).

18. By 1978, these grant-in-aid programs totaled 492. See *A Catalog of Federal Grants Funded FY 1978* (Washington: United States Advisory Commission on Intergovernmental Relations, February 1979), p. 1.

19. Jackson Pemberton, "A New Message: On Amendment XVII," *The Freeman,* November 1976, p. 657.

20. Atomic Energy Act of 1946, 60 Stat. 755, 42 U.S.C. 2011 (1947 Supp.); Atomic Energy Act of 1959, 73 Stat. 688, 42 U.S.C. 2021 (1959 Supp.).

21. Uniform Time Act of 1966, 80 Stat. 107, 15 U.S.C. 260 (1966 Supp.).

22. Water Quality Act of 1965, 79 Stat. 903, 33 U.S.C. 1151 (1965 Supp.); Air Quality Act of 1967, 81 Stat. 485, 42 U.S.C. 1857 (1968 Supp.).

23. Federal Water Pollution Control Amendments of 1972, 70 Stat. 498, 33 U.S.C. 1151 (1972 Supp.).

24. McCulloch v. Maryland, 4 Wheaton 316 (1819); Gibbons v. Ogden, 9 Wheaton 1 (1824).

25. McCulloch v. Maryland, 4 Wheaton 316 (1819).

26. Woodrow Wilson, *Congressional Government: A Study in American Politics* (Boston: Houghton Mifflin, 1925), pp. 36–37. In 1941, the United States Supreme Court broadly interpreted the commerce power in upholding the Fair Labor Standards Act of 1938 and bringing the regulation of wages and hours of labor employed in the states under federal control, thereby superseding completely state exercise of the police power in this field. See United States v. Darby, 312 U.S. 100 (1941).

27. Buckley v. Valeo, 424 U.S. 1 (1976), at 143. By implication this dictum extends to the states.

28. Ibid., at 39.

29. Ibid., at 52.

30. Ibid., at 52–53.

31. First National Bank of Boston et al. v. Bellotti, 435 U.S. 765 (1978).

32. Woodrow Wilson, *Congressional Government: A Study in American Politics,* p. 205.

33. Felix Morley, *Freedom and Federalism* (Chicago: Henry Regnery, 1959), p. 239.

34. D.W. Brogan, *Politics in America* (Garden City, N.Y.: Anchor Books, 1960), p. 228.

35. W. Brooke Graves (ed.), "Intergovernmental Relations in the United States," *The Annals,* January 1940, pp. 1–218; and Richard H. Leach (ed.), "Intergovernmental Relations in America Today," *The Annals,* November 1974, pp. 1–169. See in particular, Deil S. Wright, "Intergovernmental Relations: An Analytical Overview," pp. 1–16; Brevard Crihfield and H. Clyde Reeves, "Intergovernmental Relations: A View from the States," pp. 99–107; and Joseph F. Zimmerman, "The Metropolitan Area Problem," pp. 133–147.

36. 36 Stat. 961, U.S.C. 552 (1911).

37. *Categorical Grants: Their Role and Design* (Washington: United States Advisory Commission on Intergovernmental Relations, 1978), pp. 51–52.

38. Ibid., pp. 16 and 22.

39. G. Homer Durham, "Politics and Administration in Intergovernmental Relations," *The Annals,* January 1940, p. 5.

40. *Categorical Grants: Their Role and Design,* p. 22.

41. Ibid., p. 42.

42. Ibid., pp. 52–53.

43. Nelson A. Rockefeller, "Remarks of the Vice President at the National Governors Conference, Statler Hilton Hotel, Washington, D.C." (Washington: Office of the Vice President, February 24, 1976), p. 2 (mimeographed).

44. Florida Department of Health v. Califano, 449 F. Supp. 274, 585

F. 2d 150 (5th Cir.), *cert. denied,* 33 S. Ct. 2051 (1979). The requirement denies states flexibility in determining the organizational structure for service delivery since a state receiving a federal grant-in-aid with this condition must assign responsibility for administration of the grant program to a single discrete unit rather than to a unit that has other responsibilities even though these are related to the grant program.

45. Charles L. Schultze, "Federal Spending: Past, Present, and Future," in Henry Owen and Charles L. Schultze (eds.), *Setting National Priorities: The Next Ten Years* (Washington: Brookings Institution, 1976), p. 367.

46. James L. Buckley, "The Trouble with Federalism: It Isn't Being Tried," *Commonsense* (Summer 1978):13.

47. Ibid., p. 14.

48. *Categorical Grants: Their Role and Design,* p. 281.

49. New York Laws of 1966, chap. 478; and New York State Finance Law, sec. 53-2.

50. New York Legislature, S.7840-B and A. 10244-B of 1978.

51. "Appropriating Federal Funds in New York State," *The Ways and Means Report,* January 1977, p. 2.

52. MacManus v. Love, 499 P.2d 609 (1972).

53. Wheeler v. Barrera, 417 U.S. 402 (1973).

54. Shapp v. Casey, 99 S. Ct. 717 (1979). See also Shapp v. Sloan, Pa., 391 A.2d 596 (1978). See also George D. Brown, "Federal Funds and National Supremacy: The Role of State Legislatures in Federal Grant Programs," *American University Law Review* 28 (Spring 1979): 279-313.

55. Flammable Fabrics Act, 81 Stat. 574, 15 U.S.C. 1191 (1967 Supp.).

56. United States Grain Standards Act, 82 Stat. 769, 7 U.S.C. 71 (1968 Supp.); Sego v. Kirkpatrick, 524 P.2d 975 (1974).

57. Radiation Control for Health and Safety Act of 1968, 82 Stat. 1186, 42 U.S.C. 262 (1968).

58. Gun Control Act of 1968, 82 Stat. 1226, 18 U.S.C. 921 (1968 Supp.).

59. Drug Abuse Control Amendments of 1965, 79 Stat. 235, 21 U.S.C. 321 (1965 Supp.).

60. Federal Railroad Safety Act of 1970, 84 Stat. 972, 45 U.S.C. 151 (1970 Supp.).

61. Safe Drinking Water Act, 88 Stat. 1665, 42 U.S.C. 200g-2 (1974 Supp.).

62. Wholesome Meat Act, 81 Stat. 595, 21 U.S.C. 71 (1967 Supp.).

63. Poultry Products Inspection Act, 82 Stat. 791, 21 U.S.C. 451 (1968 Supp.).

64. Occupational Safety and Health Act of 1970, 84 Stat. 1608, 29 U.S.C. 667 (1970 Supp.).

65. Hines v. Davidowitz, 312 U.S. 52 (1941), at 67.

66. Rice v. Santa Fe Elevator Corporation, 331 U.S. 218 (1947).

67. City of Burbank v. Lockheed Air Terminal Incorporated, 411 U.S. 624 (1973), at 632.

68. Oregon v. Mitchell, 400 U.S. 112 (1970).

69. Ibid., at 126.

70. Ibid., at 128.

71. National League of Cities v. Usery, 426 U.S. 833 (1976).

72. Washington v. Davis, 426 U.S. 299 (1976).

73. Village of Arlington Heights et al. v. Metropolitan Housing Development Corporation et al., 429 U.S. 252 (1977). For a housing decision based on *Arlington Heights* dictum, see Silken v. Toledo, 558 F.2d 350 (1977); and Metropolitan School District of Perry Township v. Buckley, 429 U.S. 1068 (1977).

74. Chapman v. Houston Welfare Rights Organization, 441 U.S. 600 (1979).

75. Connecticut General Statutes Annotated, secs. 19-523 and 19-524 (1967 Supp.); New Jersey Statutes Annotated, secs. 32-29-1 to 32-29-39 (1968); and New York Public Health Law, sec. 1299-m.

76. Voting Rights Act of 1965, 79 Stat. 437, 42 U.S.C. 1973 (1965 Supp.); Voting Rights Act Amendments of 1970, 84 Stat. 314, 42 U.S.C. 1973 (1970 Supp.); and Voting Rights Act Amendments of 1975, 89 Stat. 400, 42 U.S.C. 1973 (1975 Supp.). For an analysis of the act, see Joseph F. Zimmerman, "The Federal Voting Rights Act and Alternative Election Systems," *William and Mary Law Review* (Summer 1978):621-660.

77. Perkins v. Matthews, 400 U.S. 379 (1971), at 404.

78. Brevard Crihfield and H. Clyde Reeves, "Intergovernmental Relations: A View from the States," *The Annals,* November 1974, p. 102.

79. United States Constitution, Art. III. sec. 2.

80. *Congressional Record,* February 21, 1979, p. S 1583.

81. Marjorie Hunter, "Senate, in a Surprise Move, Votes to Permit Prayer in Public Schools," *The New York Times,* April 6, 1979, p. A-14. The Senate subsequently rescinded its approval of the Helms' amendment to the administration's education department bill, but the United States House of Representatives on June 11, 1979 adopted an amendment to the education department bill allowing voluntary prayer in public schools. Marjorie Hunter, "Prayers in Schools Approved by House," *The New York Times,* June 12, 1979, p. B-20.

82. Federal Environmental Pesticide Control Act of 1972, 86 Stat. 983, 7 U.S.C. 136b (2) (1972 Supp.).

83. Clean Air Act Amendments of 1977, 91 Stat. 722, 42 U.S.C. 7424 (1977 Supp.).

84. Federal Water Pollution Control Act Amendments of 1972, 86 Stat. 841, 33 U.S.C. 1151 (1972 Supp.).

85. Emergency Highway Energy Conservation Act of 1974, 87 Stat. 1046, 23 U.S.C. 154 (1974 Supp.); and 23 C.F.R. 658.6.

86. Safe Drinking Water Act of 1974, 88 Stat. 1676, 42 U.S.C. 300h (1974 Supp.).

87. Federal Metal and Nonmetallic Mine Safety Act of 1966, 80 Stat. 783, 42 U.S.C. 2011 (1966 Supp.).

88. Wholesome Meat Act of 1967, 81 Stat. 596, 21 U.S.C. 71 (1967 Supp.); Poultry Products Inspection Act of 1968, 82 Stat. 797, 21 U.S.C. 451 (1968 Supp.).

89. National Health Planning and Resources Development Act of 1974, 88 Stat. 2242, 42 U.S.C. 300m (1974 Supp.). As part of the process of improving health services under this act, Governor Hugh L. Carey of New York on May 2, 1975 designated eight health-service areas. See *Press Release,* Albany, New York, Executive Chamber, May 2, 1975.

90. Federal Water Pollution Control Act Amendments of 1972, 86 Stat. 840 and 842, 33 U.S.C. 1151 (1972 Supp.).

91. Clean Air Act Amendments of 1977, 91 Stat. 749, 42 U.S.C. 7504 (1977 Supp.).

92. Federal Environmental Pesticide Control Act of 1972, 86 Stat. 983, 7 U.S.C. 136b (2) (1972 Supp.).

93. Surface Transportation Assistance Act of 1978, 92 Stat. 2724, 23 U.S.C. 134 (1978 Supp.).

94. National Health Planning and Resources Development Act of 1974, 88 Stat. 2247, 42 U.S.C. 300m–3 (1974 Supp.).

95. Highway Safety Act of 1966, 80 Stat. 731, 23 U.S.C. 402 (b)(1) (1966 Supp.).

96. State of New York Executive Order No. 75, April 3, 1973. The Executive Order is published in *Public Papers of Nelson A. Rockefeller: Fifty-Third Governor of the State of New York, 1973* (Albany: State of New York, n.d.), pp. 811–812.

97. Executive Order 12140 of May 29, 1979, 44 *Federal Register* 31159 (May 31, 1979). The delegation is based on the authority vested in the president by the Emergency Petroleum Allocation Act of 1973 and his inherent powers.

98. Clean Air Act Amendments of 1977, 91 Stat. 734, 42 U.S.C. 7474 (1977 Supp.).

99. Joseph F. Zimmerman, "The Metropolitan Areas Problem," *The Annals,* November 1974, p. 143.

100. Clean Air Amendments of 1970, 84 Stat. 1676, 42 U.S.C. 1857 *et seq.* 49 U.S.C. 1421 and 1430 (1970 Supp.). Previously, the United States Environmental Protection Agency in developing regulations could take into consideration the economic impact and technical feasibility of abatement controls.

101. 39 *Federal Register* 7271 *et seq.* (February 24, 1974).

102. 40 C.F.R. 52.1670 (1973). For the latest version of this plan, see *New York State Air Quality Implementation Plan: Transportation Element, New York City Metropolitan Area* (Albany: New York State Department of Environmental Conservation, December 1978).

103. Friends of the Earth v. EPA, 499 F.2d 1118 (2d Cir. 1974).

104. Clear Air Act Amendments of 1977, 91 Stat. 695, 42 U.S.C. 7410 (1977 Supp.).

105. 42 *Federal Register* 61453 (December 5, 1977).

106. Clean Air Act Amendments of 1977, 91 Stat. 722, 42 U.S.C. 7424.

107. Ibid., 91 Stat. 746–47, 42 U.S.C. 7502. Relative to the attainment of ambient air-quality standards throughout the United States, the Council on Environmental Quality in 1978 reported that only Honolulu of the 105 metropolitan areas with a population exceeding 200,000 "recorded eight consecutive quarters without a violation" of the oxidant standard which is "the criterion for attainment designation." See *Environmental Quality: The Ninth Annual Report of the Council of Environmental Quality* (Washington: USGPO, December 1978), pp. 63 and 66.

108. New York Vehicle and Traffic Law, sec. 301 (c). See also 44 *Federal Register* 70760–0763 (December 10, 1979).

109. "Smog in the Clean Air Act," *Congressional Record,* April 5, 1979, p. H2054.

110. Ibid.

111. "6 States Ask Action Against Acid Rain," *The New York Times,* January 28, 1980, p. B–1; and Lance Gay, "Carter's Environment Chief Dissents on 'Acid Rain,'" *The Washington Star,* March 20, 1980, p. A–2.

112. "Ohio Told to Meet Clean-Air Deadline," *The New York Times,* October 18, 1979, p. A–16.

113. Clean Air Act Amendments of 1977, 91 Stat. 694, 42 U.S.C. 7410. See also 45 *Federal Register* 31307–1312 (May 13, 1980); and 40 C.F.R., Parts 51–52 (1980).

114. For an example, see 45 *Federal Register* 33983 (May 21, 1980).

115. Council on Environmental Quality, *Environmental Quality— 1979* (Washington: USGPO, December 1979), p. 17.

116. See Joseph F. Zimmerman, "Mandating in New York State," *State Mandating of Local Expenditures* (Washington: United States Advisory Commission on Intergovernmental Relations, July 1978), p. 76.

4

Federal Mandates and the Future of Public Schools

Thomas H. Jones

Federal regulation of public elementary-secondary education involves a wide variety of actions by federal executive agencies, courts, and the Congress that influences the activities of local school systems. In its broadest scope the topic is massive yet amorphous, having different meanings for different people. Although federal regulation of the public schools is a popular discussion topic, it has received little serious academic treatment.

There are many things which we need to know about federal regulation. The word *regulation* is itself imprecise, referring to something as broad and momentous as an article of the Constitution or something as specific and fleeting as a remark by an HEW official to a locally employed federal grants administrator. What may be true about a regulation in general may often be mistaken in specific cases.

Second, people make claims for and against regulation. Too often, however, these claims are subjective or based on scanty evidence. It would be desirable to have more facts in order to weigh claims about the effect of regulation, pro and con.

Third, elementary-secondary education is unusual in that it has a large and heavily regulated public sector and a smaller, largely unregulated private sector. One crucial area of concern should be the intersectorial effects of regulation, both federal and state-local.

Fourth, given the fact that regulation covers such a wide variety of actions, it would be desirable to have some models available for explaining the regulatory process in elementary-secondary education. Models could be useful in understanding why we have the regulations we do and in predicting regulatory trends.

The first two sections of this chapter will address the topic of regulation from the viewpoint of an educator. The first section will deal with the extent and nature of federal regulation so that the word can be clarified for present purposes. The second section will discuss public and professional educator opinions concerning federal regulation as it exists today. The third section will present some perspectives on the facts, discussing the apparent causes and consequences of federal regulation.

The Nature and Extent of Federal Regulation

A number of books and case studies have been written on the role of the federal courts in setting educational policy, the intent and effects of specific acts of Congress, and the role of bureaus in implementing the law.[1] Here, however, the purpose is not to discuss specific measures in detail. Instead, discussion will catalogue several subject areas of school regulation to estimate their composite impact. For example, the following regulations indicate the wide variety of subjects that may emerge from any or all of the three branches of government:

1. *The Buckley amendment* protects students from disclosure of their educational records in certain cases and gives students access to most of the educational data collected about them.
2. *The Elementary and Secondary Education Act (ESEA)* funds a variety of programs, with special emphasis on poverty and minority students and bilingual programs.
3. *Special-education legislation* requires children with handicapping conditions to be diagnosed and placed in the least restrictive learning environment. Included here are federal laws requiring structural modifications of school buildings for students with physical handicaps.
4. *Title IX of the Education Amendments of 1972* bars discrimination in educational programs or activities on the basis of sex.
5. *Due process procedures* require school officials to follow specific rules and procedures in disciplinary actions.
6. *Reporting and documentation procedures* are required either as a condition for receipt of funds or as a condition for continued school operation. Frequently discussed reporting forms are those required by the Elementary and Secondary Education Act (ESEA), the Office of Civil Rights, HEW, the Occupational Safety and Health Administration (OSHA), the Employee Retirement Income Security Act (ERISA), and various routine and special reports.[2]
7. *Mandatory busing for purposes of racial balance.*

This list by no means includes every federal regulation, but it does suggest the breadth of regulation affecting instruction and teaching directly and the nature of the problems arising from these regulations.[3]

One element uniting many of these apparently disparate regulations is a concern for equity as defined by a particular law. Many of these regulations are based on specific views concerning the needs of some linguistic, racial, ethnic, or religious minority. This is the most important element in the nature of contemporary federal education regulation.

Most of the items on the preceding list concern equity in education procedures.[4] Federal regulations do not, however, attempt to dictate specific curricula content, costs, or educational performance. For example, while federal regulations require local officials to specify that some learning objectives for special-education pupils will be written, nothing in the law specifies what these objectives should be. Likewise, federal monies targeted for instruction of poor children (Title I, ESEA) and bilingual children (Title VII, ESEA) do not specify what specific skills should be taught and tested.

American federal regulation contrasts sharply with many foreign governments' education regulations, where national controls over curriculum content, expenditure, and the level of school services tend to be more complete. The basis for such regulation is the view that schools exist mainly to serve the interests of the nation as defined by central planners and policy-making bodies. In such systems, the private or local wants of individuals and communities are a secondary concern.[5] In some decentralized, federal political systems, like that of the United States, however, relationships among central governments, local governments, and individual wants are far less clear. This generalization applies to education no less than to other public enterprises.[6]

The Debate over Federal Regulation

Unlike higher education with its strong tradition of a professoriate free from political controls, the professional activities of school personnel traditionally have been regulated by external, politically chosen bodies. The current contest for control of public elementary-secondary schools cannot be viewed as one between autonomous school teachers and the "state." In reality, the contest is between different levels of government: the federal government, on the one hand, and state-local educational authorities, on the other. Traditionally, of course, the latter have done nearly all the regulating.

Federal controls on the public schools raise two major categories of debate. These may be termed debates about *philosophic principle* and debates about *extrinsic conditions*. The first category addresses the specific character of the action which the federal government requires local schools to take. For example, there are substantial disagreements about the inherent value of bilingual education, busing, prayer in school, and so forth. Objections based on extrinsic conditions go to the implications of the regulation and not the regulation itself. For example, one may feel that special programs for handicapped children are a good idea, but not feel that severely handicapped children should be placed in a regular classroom unless the teacher has either assistants or training to cope effectively.

Principled Objections to Federal Regulation

Objections based on principle are cited by citizens and educators who are concerned by what they view as intrusion of the federal government into local activities. These individuals are likely to point out that the Constitution authorizes no direct federal responsibility for public education. They often resent federal efforts to buy control through the provision of grants-in-aid, and they feel that people in the best decision-making position are the members of the roughly 15,000 local school boards in the fifty states.

Objections to federal regulation that are based on principle tend to be conceptual and abstract in nature and based on law or political theory. They emphasize dangers inherent in tampering with time-tested local methods simply to accomplish some need that seems desirable at the moment.[7] However, with the passage of time, some measure of federal intervention has itself now become the norm. Few, if any, educational leaders now oppose all forms of regulation, and such objections are no longer a major factor in political decision making.

People who accept some measure of federal control nevertheless may object to one or another federal court decision, statute, or executive department regulation. Their objection is not to the regulatory system in general, but to some specific order on which their view has not prevailed or, possibly, not even been heard.

These people may invoke "local control," but they use the phrase as a rhetorical tool to manipulate the political process. Their principal objective is to accomplish some form of deregulation, not to make an intellectual case against the system itself. Moreover, the same individual who advocates local control of education at one point in time may, at a different point, plead for federal intervention.

Principles of, and arguments for, local control abound in education literature.[8] However, this writer could find no intellectual case for a fully national centralized school system in the United States. Apparently no one advocates federal control of the public schools on principle, but only on pragmatic grounds.

Arguments for a particular federal law, judicial decision, or department of education directive are always built on the premise that, from time to time, important national priorities emerge which state-local school systems acting on their own do not meet. Local governments presumably do not share a national view, and the idea of federal regulation derives directly from this presumption. Localities must be compelled (or enticed through

funding) to carry on those activities which they would not otherwise undertake. Regulation via grant-in-aid programs is the means by which the
national government elicits local cooperation. Quite naturally in these situations, a debate ensues over just how the national interest should be defined.

In these debates "ad hocracy" reigns supreme. The lack of any over-
arching principles guiding federal education policy may explain characteristics of federal regulation already mentioned in the first section: emphasis on
special programs for target groups rather than on curriculum content or
educational effectiveness. The latter seems too directive, while the former
allows the federal government to express a social concern while minimizing
federal control over pedagogy and other traditionally local concerns. Lack
of principles guiding federal regulation of education also may explain why
attempts to consolidate grants into large blocks so as to reduce federal regulation have been politically unsuccessful. Since federal programs arise only
to meet specific problems of the poor, handicapped, and so forth, the fragmented political process dictates that each program be kept separate but
highly visible.

*Conditions Extrinsic to Federal Regulation: Conflict and
Consensus*

While some discussion about federal regulation is based on principle,
another form of discussion is based on what may be termed *extrinsic conditions.* Here it is neither the idea of regulation in general nor the broad purpose of any single regulation that is objectionable. Instead, objection is
based on some implication or side effect that makes the regulation administratively difficult and interferes with the normal operation of the school.

One claim is that regulations themselves may be written in an ambiguous way. The same regulation may be interpreted differently, and one purpose of the regulation—a uniform standard of treatment—is therefore not
achieved. These vagaries apply even to something as basic as the funding
mechanisms themselves, and the ambiguity may be exacerbated by the political culture.

> The political culture and traditions of state education politics . . . different
> in every state—determine the state distribution and administration of fed-
> eral aid. The federal-state [and local] delivery mechanism also insures that
> the implementation of policies are *not* uniform among the states.[9]

To the charge that some regulations are ambiguous, federal regulators
respond that the purpose of regulation is not to ensure completely uniform
actions in all local schools, but only to set boundaries for minimally satis-

factory operation. Local variation within the standard may be entirely appropriate in certain circumstances. Clarification of all ambiguity and elimination of all variation usually would require still further federal regulation, further limiting the freedom of local school districts. Therefore, the very uniformity sought in the application of federal regulation would be ultimately objectionable to those seeking standardization.

A second charge is that professional educators lack sufficient expertise to implement regulation effectively. For example, much regulation is enacted without considering its impact on personnel. Federal regulations often have the effect of creating an immediate shortage of qualified teachers in specific education fields. In addition, a shortage of qualified personnel tends to undermine the salutary effect of the regulation itself.

In response, it may be argued that federal programs and the resulting regulations serve to stimulate development of trained professionals to meet national needs. The argument can be made that expertise in specialized fields is lacking precisely because these areas have been neglected locally for too long. The development of expertise is a problem that will be solved over time through federal intervention, but not without it. A recent example of the need for new expertise is the special-education law requiring handicapped children to be placed in the "least restrictive environment." This necessitates training teachers to handle classrooms with both normal and slightly retarded pupils. States are now recommending special training for their teachers to meet the new need. Bilingual-education guidelines raise similar personnel problems.

Even with expertise there may be a lack of good will on the part of some federal personnel. Erratic federal enforcement provides the basis for a third objection to federal regulation on extrinsic grounds. Effective enforcement in the 15,000 local school districts of the United States is often time-consuming and costly. An anecdote offered during congressional testimony by Wilson Riles, California Superintendent of Public Instruction, makes this point:

> Recently, a principal asked a federal [Elementary and Secondary Education Act] Title I official if it were permissible to take 10 non-Title I children in a class of 30 on a field trip. The principal said it would cost no more to include the 10 youngsters on the trip planned for the 20 eligible Title I students.

> The answer was no, because "regulations" forbid non-Title I children from benefiting from Title I money. The principal asked if the district could pay for the non-Title I children. Again, the answer was no, because this would violate "comparability" requirements. [The comparability guidelines mandate comparable local expenditures for Title I and non-Title I students, thereby preventing districts from giving extra services to non-Title I students.]

The confused and frustrated principal proposed leaving the non-Title I youngsters at home. Once more the answer was no, this time because the action would amount to segregation.

The principal knew he was licked, so he asked for advice. But the federal official replied that he was not there to provide advice, just to enforce the law.

The principal said he would cancel the trip. But again the reply was no, because field trips are required to provide cultural enrichment for Title I students.

Not wanting to violate the law, the principal said, "Okay, we'll have the field trip."

The official then asked suspiciously, "How are you going to pay for it?"

"You'll never know," the principal replied with a smile and walked away.

Riles observed to the subcommittee that "people in the field who are trying to make compensatory education work should not be forced into hypocrisy."[10]

Inordinate amounts of paperwork constitute a fourth objection to federal regulation.[11] For program managers, federal regulation means completion of many intricate forms documenting compliance with the regulatory process. Such paperwork can be very time-consuming—time, it is claimed, that detracts from service to children. Rarely does the local official see any results from the information provided, and the relationship between reporting and policymaking is not well understood by most local officials. The official knows only that if reports are all right, he is unlikely to hear any more about them. If they are not satisfactory, he will get a telephone call requiring still more time and effort. Reporting thus may be viewed as a deathless chore about which no one really cares, and such attitudes hardly inspire speedy and accurate reporting on the part of local schools.

To the contention that federal mandates require too much paperwork, a response is that reporting in standard formats is essential to execute the law. Local reporting for federal programs may have several purposes of which regular national information gathering is only one. Reporting may be required so that information is available should it be needed (in a court case, for instance). Reporting may be needed to prescribe certain practices in the daily activities of local schools without actually monitoring those activities. With new federal programs the additional burden of paperwork seems heavy at first, but some teachers and administrators assert that the paperwork burden is reduced over time as local officials find less time-consuming ways to handle the reporting chore.

The preceding opinions reflect areas of conflict, but there are some aspects of federal regulation on which most people would agree. First, federal regulation has greatly altered the innovation process in education. Not many years ago innovation and reform in education were thought to begin in one locality and spread over time to others. Kindergartens, school libraries, and many other now conventional parts of public education began locally and spread to other localities over a period of decades. Today's programmatic educational innovations are likely to be spread through central-government mandate, thereby making change faster and more pervasive. For example, busing for integration, women's equity in athletics, and the ban on school prayer affected a large number of school systems at or near the same time.

Second, the regulatory process has legal and political channels to check government arbitrariness. State and local officials may be consulted in drawing the regulation. Executive branch regulations must be submitted to Congress 45 days before they become effective, and state agencies, local school districts, education organizations, and other interested parties may review and comment on regulations.[12] If anything, these channels also could be called obstacles that actually inhibit legitimate decision making.

Third, the local school districts which feel most affected by regulation are frequently reactive rather than activist. They have neither the time nor desire to become involved in federal educational policymaking. They may feel that they lack influence, or they may not foresee the effects of specific federal regulations as they are being drawn. As a result, many local officials feel powerless in influencing the federal regulatory process. Federal policymaking is viewed as a matter determined by specialized groups, including groups peripheral to the education profession.[13]

Fourth, there is agreement that there has been little empirical study of the cost-effectiveness of most federal regulations. With respect to measuring effectiveness, most regulations specify processes and not results. Education antipoverty programs are a conspicuous exception to this generality in that they have been widely studied and have been found to be generally ineffective in achieving their goal of reducing poverty through education.[14]

Fifth, from a utility-maximizing point of view, local school districts are ambivalent about federal regulatory programs. On the one hand, mandated federal programs tend to mean larger budgets and more personnel—a benefit from the local administrator's viewpoint. On the other hand, most federal education programs are not funded at their full level. Local money and school personnel may be transferred to the federally mandated program, thus forcing shifts in local priorities. Unless the perceived advantages from a partially funded program exceed the perceived disadvantages to the regular, nonfederal programs, the federal mandate is a net cost from a local educator's point of view. (However, since any individual teacher or administrator is likely to attach different values to any single federal regulation, the education establishment will generally not be of one mind about federal mandates.)

Sixth, with respect to the public generally, it seems axiomatic that the narrower the constituency for any mandate and the lower the funding level, the less popular the mandate will be. When mandates are highly unpopular and grossly underfunded, and when it is possible to avoid those mandates by transferring to a different school or school system, one would expect substantial evidence of such avoidance behavior. These aspects of conflict and consensus are explored in more detail in the following section.

The Causes and Consequences of Federal Regulation

If a policy paper were written on federal regulation of, say, the lumber industry, policymakers would be interested not just in the cost of antipollution devices and the quantity of pollutants removed from the river, but also in why regulation came about, the effects of the regulation on demand for and quantity of lumber produced, and the effects of the regulaton on the utilization of substitutes for lumber.

This section takes a similar approach with respect to public education. First, the causes of federal regulation are discussed, and then some of the indirect social costs are noted. It should be emphasized that many aspects of this discussion are highly tentative. They are based on general models of human behavior and regulatory policy and some wisps of empirical evidence. The explanations deal with what is happening and what is likely to happen, not with what should happen. In fact, this writer views some of the proposals with considerable alarm.

When the federal mandates listed in the first section of this chapter are compared with parents' perceptions of the major problems in public-school education (table 4–1), it is clear that there is little correspondence between the two lists. The inference is that federal mandates have not addressed the prime concerns of most parents. Instead, the principal motivation of regulation has been pro-poor, pro-disadvantaged, and pro-minority. The major exception to this generalization is busing for purposes of racial integration, which has been a dominant concern for both the general public and the federal government. Evidence is that far from agreeing with federal mandates, most parents are at odds with the policy.[15] The specific evidence on other federal initiatives is less clear. However, a recent poll does show that a plurality of the public believes that there is too much federal regulation generally in public education (see table 4–2).

Since the primary concerns of the majority of parents are not reflected in recent federal legislation, it is clear that to explain the causes of federal regulation in education, one must look to something other than simple majority rule. One model for examining federal behavior proposed by some political scientists is termed *interest-group liberalism*.[16] According to this explanation, public policy is set by the interactions of small but well-orga-

Table 4–1
Major Problems of Public Schools as Identified by Parents of Public and Nonpublic School Pupils

Problem	1979 Public	1979 Nonpublic	1978 Public	1978 Nonpublic	1977 Public	1977 Nonpublic	1975 Public	1975 Nonpublic	1974 Public	1974 Nonpublic
Lack of discipline	26%	32%	25%	30%	27%	29%	23%	21%	29%	32%
Segregation/integration	7	5	11	22	11	18	11	16	17	14
Lack of proper financial support	12	4	18	11	14	14	15	13	17	9
Use of drugs	14	7	13	15	6	3	9	10	15	13
Difficulty of getting "good" teachers	12	12	10	9	12	19	12	12	15	11
Size of school/classes	6	6	5	5	7	11	13	5	8	8
Parents' lack of interest	4	4	5	4	6	7	3	3	4	2
School board policies	2	—	2	—	2	—	1	2	7	2
Poor curriculum			10	18	12	14	7	5	3	7
Lack of proper facilities	2	—	2	1	3	1	3	4	3	6
Pupils' lack of interest	4	4	2	5	4	—	2	2	1	14
Poor communication	2	2	2	—	1	—	2	4	—	4

Source: Gallup Opinion Polls 1974 through 1979, as reported in *Phi Delta Kappan* (September 1974–1979).

Table 4-2
Parental Opinion on State-Federal Regulation of Public Education, 1978

	Public School Parents	Parochial School Parents
State and federal regulations help	24%	14%
Hinder	46	54
Make no difference	5	5
Don't know/No answer	25	27

Source: "Public Attitudes Toward the Public Schools, 10th Annual Gallup Poll," *Phi Delta Kappan* 60 (September 1978):41.

nized and well-financed political minorities. These interest groups act to shift governmental policies in their direction, albeit incrementally, through simultaneous exertions of identical influences on several levels and branches of government.

One corollary of this explanation is that court decisions, federal statutes, and federal-agency regulations should be viewed as instruments but not causes of federal control. Viewed in this light, regulation is not so much a legal phenomenon as a sociopolitical one. For those who want to influence governmental structures—either for more regulation or for less—the problem is not "How do we change the law?" but "How do we deal with the structure of interest-group politics?"[17]

A secondary corollary of the interest-group explanation is that regulatory change may emerge through any one of several legal mechanisms. Interest groups that are unsuccessful, or only partially successful, in one governmental arena—for example, the federal courts—are likely to make similar initiatives in other forums—for example, state courts or Congress. Assumptions about the final outcome of some regulatory initiatives may be mistaken when those assumptions are based on one test case or one piece of legislation. Instead, the same regulation is likely to surface again and again in different government arenas owing to the fact that the political model views interest groups as the true regulators. Laws and regulations are merely instruments of the regulators.

Table 4-3 proposes an interest-group model. In it, regulation has its origins among well-financed and active private political interest groups. Initial private attempts at regulation are likely to focus on state or local governments. At this early stage, the federal government is viewed as remote and intractable. However, if the interest is compelling, and if other local groups with similar interests form around the nation, the visibility of the movement grows and with it funds and membership.

At some point it becomes more cost-effective to center regulatory efforts at the federal level than to mount separate efforts in the fifty states.

Table 4–3
The Regulatory Process: An Interest-Group Model

Origins in Special-Interest Groups	Articulation through Two Media	Promulgation by One or More Branches of Government	Output
Private individuals and organizations	Advocacy medium Lobbying Testifying	Judicial	Federal mandates
Organizations and individuals communicating with government	Campaigning/ proselytizing Campaign financing	Executive	Federal mandates
	Analysis medium Problem identification Planning and prescription Writing and research Evaluation	Legislative	Federal mandates

Federal lobbying costs more, but federal action can do more in a short time to implement the mandate than years of effort in the fifty states.

Once private organizations are successful in capturing a bureau within government, federal regulation has a new and powerful ally. The public and private interests work together promoting the cause in all arenas—federal, state, local, legislative, executive, and judicial. Gains in one arena are used to solidify and promote gains in others.

Eventually, other, previously unorganized interest groups emerge claiming that the government has gone "too far." Proposals for further reform become stymied as legislative and executive arenas become centers for conflicting counterpressures. Public and private interest groups now must spend more energies protecting past successes as former allies desert the cause, believing that the gains made already are sufficient. Promoting new regulation becomes a secondary concern. The previously dynamic and youthful interest becomes "mature." Slowly the more perceptive members of mature interests realize that they will not be able to promote new gains entirely through their own efforts. Their hope now rests on exogenous shocks to the larger political system—perhaps new research, or a substantial shift in public opinion, or an innovative and sympathetic judiciary.

Special education and bilingual education would seem to represent an early mature state in the cycle of federal education regulation, while national defense education and integration/busing are in a late maturity phase.

By definition, the early mature reforms are just emerging; hence they are difficult to point out. Federal tuition tax credit plans, national pupil testing, or national regulation of teacher retirement systems are ideas whose time may yet come. When Lowi first discussed interest-group liberalism, conservative pressures in education, defined here as promoting the causes of socially advantaged groups, were quite limited. To the extent that conservative pressures existed, they were "anti" movements, such as anti-ESEA and antibusing. Despite their distrust of big government, conservatives may now be learning to use interest-group pressures to promote education regulations rather than to merely stop them. Interest-group liberalism may then simply become interest-group politics. Now everyone's into the pool; everyone, that is, with money and effective organization.

If the causes of federal regulation in public education are not well understood, the broad social consequences are still more obscure. While earlier sections of this chapter addressed the question of direct costs and benefits of federal regulation, indirect costs and secondary effects will be taken up here.

Indirect Costs of Regulation

An *indirect cost* may be thought of as an outlay that would not be measured through ordinary accounting procedures. For instance, if a local school system has to divert some of its time and money which otherwise would be spent on pupil A to a partially funded federal program for pupil B, this may be thought of as a cost of the federal program to pupil A, albeit indirect. And if, as a result of the federal program for pupil B, pupil A's education is somehow changed, this may be termed a secondary effect.

If the net result of the federal mandate (including all primary as well as secondary costs and effects) helped both pupil A and pupil B, the program would clearly be optimizing. All rational people would favor it. If the federally mandated program helped neither A nor B, the program would be anti-optimizing. Everyone would reject it. If the program benefited one pupil but not the other, a debate over equity would ensue. (In the nature of federal education mandates, it is at least conceivable that A would benefit but B would not, even if the mandate were aimed at B.) Resolution of the debate would be a matter for the political process and for more sophisticated analysis.

It is clear from the literature cited that federal regulatory policy in the past 15 years has been aimed at various target groups, especially the poor, minority, and disadvantaged.[18] If we now think of A and B as *categories* of pupils, with B being one of several different disadvantaged/poor/minority categories (for which federal regulation was designed), we can speculate about the behavior of the A class.

If the A class felt that it was being helped by the federal program aimed at B, there would be no problem. Everyone would be better off. If both A and B felt worse off as a result of a federal program, again it would be dropped, assuming an even minimally responsive political system. However, what seems to be a more accurate depiction of reality is that A believes it has been made worse off by federal programs, while various B groups support them. The evidence is only suggestive and partial, but the information in tables 4–1 and 4–2 suggest this conclusion, as does the recent behavior of the A group.

Alternative Responses to Regulation

There are three options open to the middle class, A, in the face of distasteful federal mandates. First the middle classes may move to public school districts with few members of the B groups, thereby effectively avoiding the major impact of the mandates. Second, they may remain in the same local political jurisdiction with the poor and disadvantaged groups, but reduce their discretionary local school spending to bring their costs in line with a lower level of perceived benefit from public schools. Third, the middle class may send its children to the unregulated, private school sector.

There is some evidence that all three options are taken. With respect to the exodus from the central cities, it is well documented that in many metropolitan areas families tend to move to suburbs, thereby avoiding heavy concentrations of poor, minority, and disadvantaged children attending city public schools.[19] Studies in Illinois, Michigan, and Missouri found that the school districts with largest enrollment declines were those with the greatest concentration of pupils eligible for federal antipoverty education programs.[20]

There is also evidence that some portions of the middle class are following the second option: decreasing their local financial commitment to public schools even as federal school aid is increasing. While it is by no means clear that one causes the other, it is apparent that the two phenomena are happening simultaneously in many local areas. One study of eighty-nine major central cities found that federal aid increased at two to three times the rate of local tax receipts in the 1970–1975 period. Likewise, state aid grew at a faster pace, indicating that city residents were paying a decreasing share of school costs themselves.[21] Another study, undertaken in the entirely different context of the rural South, reached the same result. There, too, increased federal aid was associated with reduced local taxes and spending.[22]

Table 4-4
Enrollments in Private Elementary-Secondary Schools as a Percentage of Total Elementary-Secondary Enrollment

Year	Percentage Private
1965 [a]	13.6
1970	10.5
1971	10.0
1972	9.9
1973	9.7
1974	10.0
1975	10.0
1976	10.1
1977 [b]	10.3
1978 [b]	10.5
1979 [b]	10.1
1980 [b]	10.8
1981 [b]	11.0
1982 [b]	11.2
1983 [b]	11.2
1984 [b]	11.2
1985 [b]	11.2
1986 [b]	11.1

Source: Adapted from the intermediate-alternative projection: *Projections of Education Statistics to 1986-1987* (Washington: National Center for Education Statistics, 1978), p. 16.

[a] This was a peak year.

[b] Projections.

The third possible response to regulation, shifting children to the private sector, seems not to be borne out by a quick glance at the enrollment data. During the mid 1960s and early 1970s, private school enrollments dropped by nearly 1 million and the percentage of all school children attending private schools dropped from 13 to 10.

However, the trend may be quite different in the next decade. Although the number of school-age children will decline, private school enrollments are expected to remain constant. Thus the proportion of all children in private schools is expected to edge slowly upward in the 1980s (see table 4-4).

The overall enrollment figures mask great changes within the private school sector itself. In recent years, Roman Catholic enrollments have declined by nearly 40 percent, while non-Catholic enrollments have increased greatly, enough to make up the entire Catholic loss. Much of the private school enrollment loss during the past decade has been in states with a heavy Catholic population, while much of the enrollment increase has been in the largely Protestant South. Table 4-5 illustrates this change. Even after allowing for movement in the overall population to the Sun Belt, rarely will such dramatic changes be observed in such a short time span.

Table 4–5
Elementary-Secondary Private School Enrollments by State, 1971–1972
and 1973–1974

State	1971–1972 Enrollment	1973–1974 Enrollment
Alabama	53	55
Arkansas	16	20
Florida	132	143
Georgia	68	80
Maryland	124	126
South Carolina	44	47
Virginia	75	85
Connecticut	101	95
Illinois	423	389
Massachusetts	189	172
New Jersey	282	Not available
New York	763	690
Pennsylvania	487	444
Wisconsin	188	176

Source: *Statistics of State School Systems 1971–1972 and 1973–1974* (Washington: National Center for Educational Statistics, 1975 and 1976), table 51, both volumes.

Experts on the phenomenon have labeled many of the new schools "protest schools."[23] Field studies have discovered that the reason for enrollment growth is not just integration and/or busing, but a variety of factors. Religious observance plays a major role in many protest schools. Private school parents also berate the public schools for poor discipline, drug and liquor use, low academic standards, and poor instruction. The major difference between private and public school parents seems not to be in the nature of the complaints, but in their financial capacity (rather than race). Affluent blacks, for example, are only about one-third less likely than affluent whites to select private schools.[24]

One of several possible explanations for these three trends—class segregation within different public schools, reduced local support for public schools in poor areas, and growing private schools in some areas—is unpopular federal mandates. Some members of the middle class may believe that their interests are not served by regulation that favors the poor, disadvantaged, and minority populations. In the North and West, where school systems tend to be organized around small suburban towns and townships, many families can escape much pro-poor regulation by moving to middle-class areas. In the South, with stricter court enforcement of desegregation and large, countywide school systems, segregation within the public school system is no longer an effective alternative. In such areas, private school enrollments grow apace.

Conclusion

The two major categories of contemporary issues in federal education policy involve more central regulation of public education and more decentralization through provision of alternatives such as vouchers or tuition tax credits.[25] These policies have been thought to stem from wholly different origins. Tax credits or vouchers are said to generate efficiency by promoting free choice; federal regulations are said to promote equity through special programs for minority racial, religious, ethnic, and educational interests.[26]

The hypothesis put forward here is that *far from being unrelated, these two policy initiatives feed upon one another.* Federal mandates not representative of majority public attitudes and only partly financed by the federal treasury have been one significant factor encouraging the middle class to "defect" from public schools made up of children representing different races and social classes. Defection may take the form of reduced discretionary local spending, increased race and class segregation within the public schools, or growth of the unregulated private sector. As public schools have become increasingly populated with children having learning difficulties, trust and confidence in the public schools have declined. Gallup polls indicate a continuing decline in ratings since 1974, the first year that the question was asked in this form (see table 4-6). As public school confidence declines, demands for more regulation increase in still another cycle. (For example, Title I ESEA was not perceived to be fully successful, so Title VII for bilingual education was passed a few years later.)

Defections to private schools build a large constituency for direct expenditure (voucher) or tax expenditure (tuition support) plans. The more defections, the less adequate the public school is seen to be and the larger the constituency for vouchers or tax credits. Many advocates of private school support are middle class; however, some liberal reformers, spokes-

Table 4-6
Ratings Given the Public Schools by the General Public

	1979	1978	1977	1976	1975	1974
A Rating	8%	9%	11%	13%	13%	18%
B Rating	26	27	26	29	30	30
C Rating	30	30	28	28	28	21
D Rating	11	11	11	10	19	16
Fail	7	8	5	6	7	5
Don't know/No answer	18	15	19	14	13	20

Source: "Eleventh Annual Gallup Poll of the Public's Attitudes Toward the Public Schools," *Phi Delta Kappan* 16 (September 1979):35.

men for the poor, are also concerned about increasingly ineffective public schools and advocate vouchers and credits. Their versions contain various pro-poor "safeguards," such as a larger voucher for slower learners.

One possible scenario would be a continuation of present trends; namely, more regulation and more objections to regulation. Conceivably this may produce congressional enactment of some private school financing plan, if the diverse interest groups can agree on a compromise. The fundamental requirement for this compromise is agreement on the extent of regulation to be imposed on the private schools. As a political force, the private schools are highly fragmented, with different groups taking opposing positions on the aid issue. This fragmentation has proved an insurmountable barrier in the past. However, their prospects would brighten considerably with further unpopular and underfunded regulation of the public school sector. More parents would defect to the private sector even without a credit, thereby building that minority interest. With further middle-class defections, dissatisfaction with the public schools is likely to continue growing.

The result of all this might be a three-sector elementary-secondary education system in the United States. One sector would be fully public, thoroughly equalized in every conceivable way, smaller than today's public sector but still enrolling a majority of children. Such public schools could be expected to enroll a disproportionate share of the poor, handicapped, and minorities. A second sector would be semipublic and semiprivate, accepting some regulation in exchange for some government financing. This might be a tuition-charging sector, but tuitions would be low enough to attract academically talented and highly motivated children from different social classes. The third sector would be fully private. This sector would fulfill the varying educational and social needs of upper-income groups and would be largely free of government regulation.

The three-sector system was for many years the British system, which tax credit and voucher advocates currently hope to emulate here.[27] Britain, however, has not been a society particularly noted in recent years either for economic growth or for social mobility. Whether the three-sector system could substantially expand opportunities for the poor, disadvantaged, and minorities is very doubtful.

Since vouchers and tax credits are unacceptable to many centralists and egalitarians, advocates of federal mandates face a dilemma. Everyone agrees that children learn a great deal from their peers. Therefore, the presence of all classes of children in the same school building is highly desirable. The more successful that reformers are in extending pro-poor reform, however, the less likely it will be that public schools can retain a heterogeneous population. The dilemma becomes particularly acute when the reforms themselves are based on questionable pedagogical or sociological assumptions. In the worst possible case, all pro-poor reforms are antioptimizing in the sense discussed earlier. The poor are not helped and the middle class exits. Both categories A and B are losers.

This section has speculated about the indirect social costs of federal regulation of elementary-secondary education. On the positive side there may be some indirect social benefits. Federal mandates clearly have brought many educational services to children who would not ordinarily have received them, and some children have benefited in terms of improved vocational and academic skills.[28] However, beyond this, it is difficult to find other benefits.

In this context, it is interesting to note that Gallup polls describe a consistent decline in the public's expression of racial prejudice since such events as the *Brown* and *Swann* decisions and passage of ESEA Title I.[29] The least overtly prejudiced groups within society are those who have graduated from school most recently and those who have obtained the most formal schooling. Yet during recent years, the public has consistently mentioned integration as one of the public school's biggest problems. One might conclude that using the public school as an arena for resolving social conflict has had some positive long-range and indirect social benefits, although the public schools themselves have by no means participated in that benefit.

Recommendations

The following suggestions are made for the purpose of rectifying the more dysfunctional aspects of federal regulation:

1. *Costs and benefits of regulation.* An observation made at the beginning of this chapter was that little is known about federal regulation. To remedy this matter, Congress should authorize empirical investigation of the costs and benefits of regulation in public education. Topics that might profitably be investigated are

a. The role of private and governmental interest groups in promoting regulation.
b. The direct costs of regulation, determining the extent to which federal grants meet the full costs.
c. The direct benefits of regulation, determining the long-range salutory effects for those disadvantaged groups which regulation is intended to help.
d. The indirect costs and benefits of federal education regulation, the effects of regulation upon levels of financial support for the public schools and the school choice, and the effects of regulation on public school curriculum and on parent-teacher attitudes.

2. *Funding of federal education mandates.* As indicated earlier, when federal mandates are not fully funded, resources and personnel from more popular local programs may be diverted to cover the costs of these frequently unpopular federal requirements. The possible result is public dissatisfaction with local schools. Parents with the economic means may defect to other schools, public or private, and successfully avoid the mandates. Yet the mandates require middle-class participation in order to be effective. This argues, at minimum, for full funding of every federal mandate. The advisability of mandates without generous funding is questionable; without funding, pro-poor/minority/disadvantaged mandates may be self-defeating.

3. *The federal aid to private schools issue.* Most of the debate on the issue has centered around church-state relations, individual rights, and public school monopoly theories. The question of federal regulation of schools receiving tax credit or voucher pupils has not been discussed in depth.

It should be discussed. Clearly one reason for private schools is avoidance of federal, as well as state and local, regulation. If the federal government provides subsidies to private schools but no regulation, the government will thwart its own regulatory policies. If heavy bureaucratic regulation becomes the quid pro quo for private school funding, some of the efficiency arguments for private schools will have to be reconsidered.

4. *Federal schools for the nation's largest cities.* Despite the recent regulatory efforts of the federal government, public schools for the poor child and the urban child are often very ineffective. One possible experiment would be to establish a free middle school–high school in each of several large cities across the United States. The federal schools should be models of what the majority of the public wants its schools to be. That is, the federal schools should emphasize high academic and disciplinary standards. Large cities would be an appropriate location for such schools because of their currently heavy financial and educational burdens. Admission to the federal school should be selective, based on the criteria mentioned earlier. Suspension or expulsion from these schools to other public schools should only be a last resort available to the school staff, however.

Applying these criteria would be likely to produce schools containing a disproportionate percentage of white and middle-class children, at least in their first few years of operation. Such schools might be termed racist and elitist by some because many prominent educational leaders feel that schools enrolling only the bright, honest, and motivated are irrelevant to the problems of urban education.

The response is that fair degrees of student ability and discipline are essential prerequisites for schools to work well, given our present understanding of the educational process. Private schools in cities should not have a monopoly on excellence.

There would be several advantages to such a plan. Many children from poor and disadvantaged families would have an opportunity for a good education, an opportunity now often denied them unless they can get a private school scholarship. The public schools would retain a larger proportion of urban middle-class children and could solicit the interest of more middle-class parents in public education. Finally, such schools would be a model challenging all city schools and city children to excellence.

5. *The role of minority interest groups in the formation of federal education policy.* The third section of this chapter argued that most federal education policies reflect the interests of small, well-organized interest groups. One approach to this problem would be to reduce the benefits of national lobbying by insisting, where possible, that regulation be applied selectively. Where feasible, education regulation should be tried first in test areas of the country. Evaluations would be done to determine the success of the field experiment.

Field experiments are a sound method in social science, and they may provide the only scientific means for appraisal of specific new regulations. However, they do not fit well with the American political-legal system, which is geared to providing identical treatment to everyone. The argument against the selective-experimental approach to regulation would be that governments cannot experiment with basic rights and opportunities. The response is that the novelty of the regulation, the complexity of its implementation, and its uncertain effects argue for a moderate approach.

Experimentation would not be feasible in the case of every regulation, but the experimental approach would have three political benefits. Politicians could appear to accede to the wishes of even more special interests, but on an experimental basis. This would fulfill politicians' needs while not requiring large sums from the federal treasury. (Demonstration programs should be generously funded, however.) Interest groups themselves would tend to focus more attention outside Washington, since federal successes would be provisional and complete victory could occur only well into the future, when the experiment was proven to be successful.

Pressures on Washington officials would diminish, and the general public would have time to adjust to the new regulation as evidence became available that the regulation was successful. If such an approach had been applied in the case of, say, special education or bilingual education, it is likely that all parties would have benefited.

During the past two decades, public school policy has been influenced by diverse interest groups, each trying to mandate its own particular vision for the future. In some respect social reform has replaced socialization as the principal purpose of schools. The preceding recommendations are designed to reduce, although not eliminate, the diverse pressures for mandated reform. With pressures reduced, schools could better fulfill the social purpose for which they are uniquely fitted: transmission of the existing national culture to the next generation, to change as *they* see fit.

Notes

1. See, for example, Stephen K. Bailey and Edith K. Mosher, *The Office of Education Administers a Law* (Syracuse: Syracuse University Press, 1968; Gary Orfield, *Must We Bus?* (Washington: Brookings Institution, 1978); Jerome T. Murphy, *State Education Agencies and Discretionary Funds* (Lexington, Mass.: Lexington Books, D.C. Heath, 1974; and Andrew Fishel and Janice Potter, *National Politics and Sex Discrimination in Education* (Lexington, Mass.: Lexington Books, D.C. Heath, 1977).

2. The Illinois State Superintendent of Education counted more than two dozen such special reports in the 1970–1975 period. See Joseph M. Cronin, "The Federal Takeover: Should the Junior Partner Run the Firm?" *Phi Delta Kappan* 57 (April 1976):500.

3. For example, OSHA standards affect school building and conditions of work. ERISA regulates school district retirement planning for many of their noninstructional personnel. And Agriculture Department policies affect school lunch programs.

4. Some federal law appears to be aimed at efficiency concerns, for example, career education and metric education. See Michael T. Timpane, *The Federal Interest in Financing Schooling* (Cambridge, Mass.: Ballinger, 1978), p. XIV.

5. Not surprisingly, the most complete statist philosophies of education are associated with totalitarian political systems. See, for example, the discussion of the German educator Paul Natorp in Jordan DeHoure's, *Philosophy and Education* (New York: Benzinger Brothers, 1930); or Lu Ting-Yi "Education Must be Combined with Productive Labor," in Mary Alice White and Jan Duker (eds.), *Education, A Conceptual and Empirical Approach* (New York: Holt-Rinehart, 1973), pp. 41–46. In more moderate political systems the debate over centralized planning tends to center as much on empirical questions as ethical ones. See George Psacharopoulos, "Investment in Education and Equality of Opportunity" in *Educational Need in the Public Economy* (Gainesville, Fla.: Univ. of Florida, 1976), pp. 35–63; and Josef M. Ritzen, *Education, Economic Growth and Income Distribution* (New York: Elsevier North-Holland, 1977).

6. David R. Cameron and Richard I. Hofferbert, "The Impact of Federalism on Education Finance: A Comparative Analysis," *European Journal of Political Research* 2 (1974):225–258.

7. See, for example, Robert M. Hutchins, *The Conflict in Education in a Democratic Society* (New York: Harper, 1975).

8. Charles M. Tiebout, "A Pure Theory of Local Expenditures," *Journal of Political Economy* 64 (October 1956):416–417; Paul Mort and Francis Cornell, *Adaptability of Public School Systems* (New York: Bureau of Publication, Teachers College, Columbia University, 1938); and Thomas H. Jones, "The Case for Local Control," *Journal of Education Finance* 2 (Summer 1976):110–122.

9. Michael W. Kirst, "Federal Aid to Public Education: Who Governs?" in Joel S. Berke and Michael W. Kirst (eds.), *Federal Aid to Education* (Lexington, Mass.: Lexington Books, D.C. Heath, 1972), p. 65.

10. Noted in Paul Copperman, *The Literacy Hoax* (New York: William Morrow, 1978).

11. *Paperwork Problems in Elementary and Secondary Education,* hearings before the Subcommittee on Elementary, Secondary and Vocational Education of the Committee on Education and Labor House of Representatives, May 1977, p. 1.

12. Cronin, "The Federal Takeover."

13. Joel H. Spring, "The Crisis in Government School Finance," *Inform* 2 (2).

14. See Henry M. Levin, "A Radical Critique of Education Policy," *Journal of Education Finance* 3 (Summer 1977):26; and Harvey A. Auerch et al., *How Effective is Schooling?* (Sonta Monica, Calif.: Rand Corporation, 1972).

The author estimates administrative costs of federal regulation of public schools to be $520 million in FY 1979. In preparing the estimate, I assumed that (1) all federal education programs involve regulation, and (2) the administrative costs are the same proportion of federal education programs as they are of all education programs:

$$C = \frac{AD}{B}$$

where C = the administrative costs of federal programs

    A = estimated total expenditures for school administration, 1979, $3.458 billion

    B = estimated total expenditure for all school operations, 1979, $72.1 billion

    D = estimated federal budget authorization for public schools, 1979, $10.862 billion

Data items A and B are found in *Digest of Education Statistics, 1979* (National Center for Education Statistics, Washington: USGPO, 1978), p. 76; and *Projections of Education Statistics to 1986–7* (National Center for Education Statistics, Washington: USGPO, 1978), p. 90. Data item D was calculated by David W. Brenneman, "Education" in Joseph Pechman (ed.) *Setting National Priorities* (Washington: Brookings Institute, 1978). The authorization exceeds the actual congressional appropriation by about $1 billion. However, the authorized figure may be a more realistic figure on which to base administrative costs, since federal programs must be fully administered even if they are not fully funded.

Solving the equation leads to a figure of $521 million for federal regulatory administrative costs in education, FY 1979.

Other available data indicate that this estimate may be conservative. The U.S. Office of Education stated that in 1973 the paperwork connected with federal elementary and secondary education required 2.2 million staff hours and 43.4 million separate data items. By contrast, 50 state and 15,000 local agencies together required only 11.2 million data items and 0.7 million person hours of paperwork. It should be kept in mind, however, that reporting is only one relatively small aspect of regulation and that state-local reporting requirements would be likely to grow somewhat if federal requirements were diminished.

15. Gary Orfield, *Must We Bus?* p. 114.

16. Theodore J. Lowi, *The End of Liberalism: Ideology, Policy and the Crisis of Public Authority* (New York: Norton, 1969).

17. Eugene Eidenberg and Roy D. Morey, *An Act of Congress: The Legislative Process and the Making of Education Policy* (New York: Norton, 1969); Dale Mann, "Public Understanding and Education Decision-Making," *Educational Administration Quarterly* 16 (Spring, 1974): 1–18; and for a more general discussion of interest groups, see Robert A. Dahl and Charles E. Lindblom, *Politics, Economics and Welfare: Economic Systems Resolved into Basic Social Processes,* (New York: Harper and Row, 1953;, especially chapters 10 and 11.

18. Timpane, *The Federal Interest;* Joel S. Berke and Michael W. Kirst (eds.), *Federal Aid to Education* (Lexington, Mass.: Lexington Books, D.C. Heath, 1972); and Fishel and Potter, *National Policies and Sex Discrimination.*

19. James S. Coleman et al., *Trends in School Segregation, 1968–73* (Washington: Urban Institute, 1975); R.L. Green and T.F. Pettigrew, "Public School Desegregation and White Flight: A Reply to Professor Coleman," *Harvard Educational Review* 46 (Winter 1976):1–53; and Christine H. Rossell, "School Desegregation and White Flight," *Political Science Quarterly* 90 (Winter 1975–96):675–695.

20. G. Alan Hickrod, *Enrollment Change and Educational Personnel Change in K-12 Schools of Illinois* Normal, Illinois (Center for the Study of Education Finance, 1976); and Allen Odden and Phillip Vincent, *The Fiscal Impacts of Declining Enrollments in Four States: Missouri, Michigan, South Dakota and Washington* (Denver: Education Commission of the States, 1976).

21. The decline in local school taxes relative to federal aid is documented in John J. Callahan, Seymour Sacks and William H. Wilken, *Big City Schools 1970-75, A Profile of Changing Fiscal Pressures* (Washington: National Conference of State Legislatures, 1977).

22. Joel D. Sherman et al., "Underfunding of Majority Black School Districts in South Carolina," School Finance Project, Lawyer's Committee for Civil Rights under Law, Washington, D.C.; October 1977. For information on historic trends documenting the relative decline in city school spending and the rise in suburban school spending see Seymour Sacks, *City Schools/Surburban Schools* (Syracuse, N.Y.: Syracuse Univ. Press, 1972), pp. 28-37.

23. David Nevin and Robert E. Bills, *The Schools that Fear Built: Segregationist Academies in the South* (Washington: Acropolis Books, 1976).

24. Office of Technology Assessment, *A Preliminary Analysis of Demographic Trends in Influencing the Elementary and Secondary School System* (Washington: United States Congress, 1977), p. 300. See also Donald Erickson, Richard L. Nault, and Bruce S. Cooper, *Recent Enrollment Trends in U.S. Non-Public Schools: Final Report to the National Institute of Education* (Washington: N.I.E., 1977).

25. M. Friedman, *Capitalism and Freedom.* (Chicago, Ill.: Univ. of Chicago Press, 1962), chapter VI; and Walter I. Garms, James W. Guthrie, and Lawrence C. Pierce, *School Finance* (Englewood Cliffs, N.J.: Prentice-Hall, 1978), pp. 18-43.

26. See James A. Maxwell and Bernard L. Weinstein, "A Tax Credit for Certain Education Expenses," in *Tax Credits for Education* (Washington: President's Commission on School Finance, 1971), pp. 1-22; and Donald Erickson, *Public Controls for Non-Public Schools* (Chicago: Midwest Administration Center, University of Chicago, 1969).

27. Britain has recently done away with the middle sector. Most of the schools within that sector opted to become fully tuition-supported schools. Pressures in support of the middle sector, however, are still strong and a Conservative Parliament could revive it, although Prime Minister Margaret Thatcher had not done so as of early 1980.

28. Levin, "A Radical Critique," pp. 9-31.

29. *The Gallup Poll: Public Opinion 1972-77* (Wilmington, Delaware: Scholarly Resources, Inc., 1978), p. 180.

5 The Political Dynamics of Intergovernmental Policymaking

Cynthia Cates Colella with
David R. Beam

Whether the nation is in the midst of good times or bad, war or peace, inflation or recession, three themes inevitably emerge in campaign years: defense
preparedness, the state of the economy, and the size of the federal bureaucracy. Depending on the times and the candidates, of course, our defense
preparedness will be alleged either to be in a state of slight strategic imbal-
ance or so low as to invite Soviet aggression; the economy either a little
shaky or in a state of crisis; and the federal bureaucracy either somewhat
bloated or grossly obese.

Neither first-strike capability not the Consumer Price Index will be
discussed here. Rather, we will begin with the assertion that (1) contrary to
popular belief, the federal bureaucracy has not grown out of control. Moreover, the first assertion is true because (2) federal policy objectives have
been accomplished largely through intergovernmental devices; in other
words, through the "marbleization" of almost every national and a great
many parochial concerns.[1] Finally, (3) this "marbleization" has occurred
through the complex interplay of a variety of political actors and forces.

Growing by Grants and Regs: The Broadening and Deepening of Federal Influence

Over the past two decades much has been made of the mushrooming of
federal expenditures. Yet, of equal if not greater consequence than the budgetary colossus has been the ever-increasing breadth and depth of the so-
called federal leviathan. It is a functional breadth that manifests itself in
federal program concerns ranging from pothole repairs to jellyfish control
and a jurisdictional depth that has distinguished itself in the past 20 years by
an unprecedented tendency to participate in, if not to intrude upon, more
and more state and local activities.

Far from bloating its own bureaucracy to carry out its own initiatives,
the accomplishment of federal policies and national goals has hinged upon
the rapid expansion of conditional grants-in-aid and regulations, adminis-

Portions of this chapter summarize material from the ACIR's recent study, *The Federal Role
in the Federal System*.

131

tered by states and localities and, in many cases, paid for by state and local taxes.

This tendency to "intergovernmentalize" has served at least three significant purposes. First, it has allowed the federal government to expand its activities without engaging in the politically unwise practice of increasing the number of its employees. While state and local employment has boomed, the size of the federal bureaucracy has actually been declining since the late 1960s.[2]

Second, it has allowed the federal government to pass on significant costs to other levels of government. As a rule, initiation of both grants-in-aid and regulations is accomplished in a "pass now, pay later" atmosphere, the eventual outcome of which sees much of the "paying" done by other than the "passer."[3]

Finally, the attachment to grants-in-aid of conditions or requirements, either program-specific or crosscutting, has allowed the federal government to accomplish a number of national policy and administrative objectives while avoiding both the political appearance of and constitutional prohibitions against federal coercion.[4]

This is not to suggest any conspiratorial activity on the part of federal policymakers, the aim of which is to overburden the nation's governors, mayors, and county commissioners. On the contrary, far from the care and planning that feeds successful conspiracies, such policy has been created with the carelessness of a random shot. Policy initiation, more often than not, results from a kind of benevolent ignorance—a well-intentioned commitment to goals rather than to practical outcomes or costs. In addition, far from a tightly knit cabal, those supporting such policies and policymaking have been a host of Washington "insiders" and "outsiders," including the nation's governors, mayors, and county commissioners.

The remainder of this chapter, examining the "whos and whats" of grants and regulations, is based on research done for a recent study of the federal role in the federal system by the Advisory Commission on Intergovernmental Relations. The bulk of this research focused on a series of case studies examining public assistance (both categorical cash programs and food stamps), unemployment, higher education, elementary and secondary education, environmental protection, libraries, and fire protection. While these functional areas comprise only a fraction (albeit a substantial fraction) of the federal government's current business, they nonetheless provide insight into a wide and representative range of grant-in-aid and regulatory endeavors, from the massive to the miniscule, from the obviously national to the traditionally local. Each of these case studies was designed to illustrate the overall dynamics of the policy process and thus to determine which of a variety of political, economic, and social forces "caused" the existing "marbleized" dimensions of government.

Two broad types of policy-producing and policy-shaping variables—policy actors and environmental influences—were examined in the case studies. The policy actors included both traditional institutional entities and external or noninstitutional entities. Hence Congress, the President, the bureaucracy, the courts, the press, public opinion, elections, political parties, and that vast and rapidly swelling army of the "actively concerned" known as interest groups were all scrutinized for their effect on and contribution to the increasing intergovernmental depth of the federal government. Social/demographic trends and dislocations such as war and economic aberrations constituted the environmental influences or forces. If, as some claim, government has gone awry, if the "enumerated powers" of 1789 have become the immeasurable activities of 1980, if the sublime ideal has become, to public and officeholder alike, a subliminal nightmare, all these actors and forces are—to a greater or lesser extent—responsible.

The Policy Actors

The realm of policymaking in the aforementioned case studies was distinguished by its complexities and circularities. Explanations of the current scope and shape of government that place almost total responsibility on a self-aggrandizing bureaucracy or a headline-grabbing presidency or an insidious network of special interests confuse far more than they enlighten. Thus the study presented a description of the policy process and an explanation for program inception and growth which, of necessity, is far more complex than much of the existing literature would suggest, for in the policy arena there is no one determinative factor—only the constant responses of a variety of political actors to each other and to the forces that define their environment.

Policymaking and the "Inside" Player

Amid this complex interplay, however, certain actors are distinguished by larger-than-life roles. By virtue of proximity alone, the so-called Washington insider would, at least, be expected to have a leading edge in the expansion of the federal government. In this case, Washington insiders or inside players include traditional institutional actors—Congress, the President, the bureaucracy, and the Court—as well as interest groups. Indeed, we found that some, but not all, of these insiders were among the major forces responsible for government growth. Indeed, if one actor, inside or outside, has been the most consistently responsible, that actor is Congress.[5]

The Congressional Policy Role

Inasmuch as ours is a growing government "of laws and not of men," the statutory expansion of the national government obviously hinges on the institutional Congress. In the realm of gross statistical possibilities, today's floor vote has a 50-50 chance of becoming tomorrow's public law. Yet floor votes, arguably, are of secondary importance to a complex, sometimes enigmatic policy process. Rather, it is another side of Congress—the individual as opposed to the institutional—that, among all the actors and forces contributing to the current scope of intergovernmental policy, has loomed largest in the sphere of policy initiation. It is the individual member of Congress, manifesting himself or herself in the role of policy entrepreneur, who has had the most profound and persistent influence on the growth of government.

Policy Entrepreneurship

The policy or public entrepreneur, not unlike his or her counterpart in the private sector, assumes responsibility for a venture—in this case, a particular project, program, or policy. In assuming such responsibility, the entrepreneur becomes the venture's chief advocate and activist. The motives of these entrepreneurs or issue activists, the size and scope of their undertakings, and the eventual impact of their promotional efforts may differ dramatically. Yet one fact is clear: in each of the cases studied, public entrepreneurship of one sort or another—congressional, presidential, bureaucratic, or special interest—was the predominant factor in policy genesis and maturation. Moreover, in every case, only Congress played a consistently crucial role, and in all but one of these program areas, the congressional role was manifest most often not in institutional form, but in the form of Congress as separate individuals—in other words, through congressional entrepreneurship.

The congressional entrepreneur may be a powerful committee or subcommittee chairman with ready access to strategic support, or he or she may be a struggling freshman with little immediate backing beyond an inexperienced staff and far-away constituency. Moreover, entrepreneurs may choose to pursue single programs, broad regulations, or entire policy areas. In addition, while the congressional entrepreneur is generally the political horse leading a cartful of interests, occasionally the cart may nudge the horse into a trot, if not a full gallop. Finally, entrepreneurship may be a solo undertaking, a joint venture, or a struggle among incipient supporters competing for a portion of the glory attached to a successful and popular policy or program.

A final phenomenon relating to national policy, particularly congressional, entrepreneurs is their tendency to use rather narrow intergovernmental devices for achieving their purposes. This tendency is manifest most clearly in the congressional preference for conditional categorical grant programs as opposed to direct national programs or the broader, less conditional block-grant approach. Three distinctly political characteristics contribute to this predilection of Congress.

In the first place, the political aspirations of individual members of Congress contribute to the narrow intergovernmental approach in two ways: narrow categorical programs "provide more opportunities for sponsorship:"[6]

> ... by and large constituents are more interested in a Congressman's ability to serve in a material way than in his/her competence in broad policymaking or the rightness of positions on issues of principle, form or structure. Such service is more easily personalized and made visible to the electorate by sponsoring or supporting specific narrow (categorical) programs than by championing a more general (block grant) approach.[7]

In the second place, the decentralization of Congress contributes to this approach because the committee and subcommittee structure of Congress favors narrow intergovernmental programs:

> Problems addressed by a potential grant program tend to be defined within the functional (and subfunctional) jurisdiction of an individual subcommittee, encouraging the narrow categorical approach to problem solving rather than the broader more integrated . . . approach.[8]

This same structure makes individual committees and committee members more vulnerable to interest-group pressures that generally favor more narrow intergovernmental programs.

Finally,

> Because power is so decentralized, [Congressional leaders] cannot rely very heavily on their hierarchical authority, party loyalty, and party discipline in mustering support for desired legislation. They have to use their negotiation resources, such as a promise of support for a member's pet project or program in exchange for a vote in favor of a measure that the leaders are seeking to promote.[9]

Congressional Entrepreneurship: Policy Initiation. There are many times when program persistence—a sort of congressional combination of loyalty, fortitude, and "pestiness"—pays off in terms of statutory realization. Among the ACIR case studies, the clearest example of such persistence was found in the Food Stamp Program and its champion, Representative Leonor K. Sullivan.

Indeed, for Sullivan, the Food Stamp Program was a sort of legislative raison d'etre. Waging an almost quixotic battle against the steadfastly opposed Eisenhower administration, Republican members of Congress, hostile committee chairmen, and rural and southern reticence, Sullivan, an Agriculture Committee outsider, waited 10 years for the opportunity to log-roll her bill into law. Thereafter, the Missouri congresswoman continued to fight against unfriendly amendments and bargain for favorable provisions.

The impetus for Sullivan's uphill entrepreneurship was pervasive mal-nourishment among her constituency, residents of a poor district in St. Louis. In a similar vein, the stimulus for Senator Paul Douglas' sponsorship of the Area Redevelopment Act (ARA), the progenitor of structural unem-ployment and manpower programs, was the "hard core" unemployment found in southern Illinois in the 1950s. In fact, Sullivan's food stamp quest bore a number of striking similarities to Douglas's 6-year pursuit of ARA.

A different characterization of the persistent sponsor was provided by Senator Warren Magnuson and his role in the creation and passage of the Fire Prevention and Control Act of 1974. Magnuson, a member of the Senate since 1944, possessed neither the underdog qualities of Douglas nor Sullivan's goal fixation. Nevertheless, Magnuson did translate an interest in consumerism into an intense fire-protection advocacy and became the driving force behind a federal role in local fire prevention and control.

Obviously, responding to one's constituency in the form of needed social programs or pork barrel projects is its own reward, and that type of entrepreneurship is probably most common. However, congressional entre-preneurs by no means confine themselves to legislative tangibles. Regula-tion, steeped as it often is in lofty goals, symbolic rhetoric, and instant national press attention, may also present itself as a golden entrepreneurial opportunity. Such regulatory entrepreneurship has been prevalent in federal education policy in recent years.

One of the clearest examples of congressional issue activism in the regu-latory arena appeared in the case of Title IX of the Education Amendments of 1972, which seeks the elimination of sexually discriminatory practices in educational admissions, facilities, and practices. Authored and championed by Representative Edith Green, Title IX resulted from the Oregon congress-woman's discovery of the existence of sexual bias in many, if not most, institutions of learning. Enlisting the support of women's groups and sympathetic female congressional staffers, Green was successful in her endeavor despite the fact that it lacked any interest or support from the educational community.

While it is not surprising that a female member of Congress would sponsor an antidiscriminatory amendment, one of the most controversial education regulatory laws was born of a very unusual source. An outstanding case of pure congressional entrepreneurship, the Family Educational Rights and Privacy Act of 1974 (FERPA), sponsored by Senator James Buckley, was adopted in spite of the fact that it "had not been the subject of Congressional hearings" and "professional educators were not involved in drafting the original legislation nor even aware of its existence."[10]

Overall, the federal regulatory role in elementary, secondary, and higher education has been a congressional innovation. Thus to the ranks of FERPA and Title IX may be added section 504 of the Rehabilitation Services Act, which prohibits discrimination against the handicapped by federal grant recipients and the Education for All Handicapped Children Act. Each of these, along with other far-reaching regulatory enactments, was created, initiated, and pursued by congressional entrepreneurs.

Policy Escalation and Multientrepreneurship. In the private marketplace, entrepreneurship is generally thought of as a highly competitive process—as a rule, for every McDonald's there is a Burger King. In Congress, however, entrepreneurial competition manifests itself less often as a "battle among the cheeseburgers" than as a rivalry among any number of different legislative proposals, each vying for a place on the crowded legislative agenda. Nonetheless, genuine competition over similar or identical issues does occur even on Capitol Hill. The most striking example of this sort of policy contention was found in the area of environmental protection.

The first stage of environmental policymaking, lasting until approximately 1969, was dominated by just a few entrepreneurs within Congress, most notably former Senator Edmund Muskie. Thus, Muskie, Chairman of the Senate Subcommittee on Air and Water Pollution, was almost entirely responsible for the development and passage of the air-pollution acts of 1965 and 1967 as well as for the water-pollution acts of 1965 and 1966. In the nature of a policy entrepreneur, he shaped each successive piece of legislation, slowly enhancing his own role while making incremental changes in the policy over which he held sway.

Unlike the first stage, the second stage of the environmental policymaking process, beginning in 1969, involved more congressional entrepreneurs and supportive interests. As public interest in the environment intensified and expanded, the number of actors directly involved in the process also increased. In addition, policymakers began reacting not only to their own perceptions of public demands, but also to the proposals of other policymakers. Hence environmental policy came to be made in what was essentially an atmosphere of one-upmanship.

Inevitably, Senator Muskie was once again the pivotal figure; in order to retain his position as chief environmental policymaker, he was forced to react to each new actor who entered the process. Having watched his proposed National Air Quality Standards Act be eclipsed by Senator Henry Jackson's *National Environmental Policy Act,* sweeping presidential environmental policy statements, broad proposals by a number of members of the House of Representatives, the media-successful Earth Day demonstration sponsored by Senator Gaylord Nelson, and an extremely critical Nader report, Muskie was literally forced to come up with something bigger and better or relinquish his leadership role. His choice was reflected in the *Clean Air Act of 1970,* a radical departure from the incrementalism of prior environmental legislation.[11]

Program Growth and the Institutional Congress: The Special Case of Welfare

Among the cases studied, only one lacked any apparent congressional entrepreneurship. Even in this case, however, Congress loomed largely as the principal policy actor, not in an individual but in an institutional sense.

Categorical cash public assistance, Aid to Families with Dependent Children (AFDC) and Supplemental Security Income (SSI), does not easily lead itself to the entrepreneurial drive. It would be an odd elected official indeed who wished to proclaim to the world that "I made welfare grow." Yet two major factors have been responsible for the tremendous long-term growth of cash public assistance: an open-ended appropriation based on federal matching for state spending and the institutional Congress.

Although incremental in nature, the congressional welfare role, characterized by benefit increases, formula adjustments, and a sometimes near fatalistic response to state spending patterns, has contributed significantly to government growth and increasing intergovernmental complexities. However, congressional control of public assistance is notable not for individual entrepreneurial support nor firm group advocacy, but rather for its ambivalence. Congress "captured" welfare policy. Its initiation as part of the Social Security Act was a clear case of presidential entrepreneurship, and Congress has retained its control of public assistance because aid to the elderly has been a popular program. As part and parcel, it inherited a small program of aid to dependent children, a program along with old-age assistance that was supposed to all but wither away, and therein lay the seeds of congressional ambivalence.[12] It is an ambivalence that allows the collective Congress to deplore the rise of the "welfare state" while enacting upward formula adjustments as a means of providing fiscal relief to the states, to decry the "welfare explosion" while resisting presidential pleas for decreased spending, and to speak often of "welfare reform" but to thwart its actual passage. Hence, whatever its liabilities or assets, the primary factor in the federal role in public assistance is the institutional Congress.

In the creation of intergovernmental policy and the programmatic growth of government, the congressional role, particularly in its entrepreneurial manifestation, has been paramount. Yet, as aesthetically and intellectually compelling as this simple answer is, it fails to offer more than a partial explanation. Congress may be chief among those who make government grow, but it has been often profoundly influenced by other policy actors.

The Interest-Group Policy Role

In simpler times, the term *interest group* conjured up a threefold image: big business, organized labor, and a somewhat amorphous farm movement. Each had its cabinet-level department, each could count on a number of strong congressional defenders and detractors, and two represented major support for the political parties with which they were identified. Not so many years ago, it was a truism that "for every broad sector there is an interest group." Today it is equally true to assert that "for every possible interest there is a group."

Indeed, there is no doubt that special interests have blossomed or perhaps exploded into a major political force. A recent edition of the *Congresssional Record* exhibited an astonishing 100-page listing of registered Washington lobbying organizations, including lobbyists not only for major businesses, organized labor, and farm groups, but also for (among many others) nonprofit citizen and environmental groups, professional associations, research institutes, Indian tribes, ethnic fraternities, sports players' leagues, foreign governments, and American municipalities.[13]

Yet, for all their notoriety and multitude, interest groups have tended to play a secondary, albeit a profoundly significant, role in the policy process. The importance of such groups very often lies not in their greatly exaggerated abilities to create and successfully advocate new policies, but rather in the ability of policies to sustain new interest groups. Once established, a group will inevitably work to sustain the policy that gave it life. If policy is primarily "created" by Congress, to interest groups, the "offspring" of policy, accrues its "care and feeding."[14]

The Resultant Interest and Second-Generation Policy

In the policy process, a common scenario is the creation of a program through congressional entrepreneurship; in turn, this program or policy will itself give birth to a policy niche—in other words, to form its own small space among the vast array of government endeavors. Interested groups (usually program beneficiaries) will generally rush to fill this niche. Once firmly established, these "resultant interests" will, quite rationally, act to perpetuate, enlarge, and add on to the policies that give them a clear advantage.[15]

Since the heightening of federal environmental activity in the late 1960s and enactment of the National Environmental Policy Act (NEPA) in 1969, the number of interest groups concerned with environmental issues has grown dramatically. Thus, older conservation groups such as the Sierra Club were joined in the battle for antipollution regulations and enforcement by such groups as the Natural Resources Defense Council, founded in 1970 in response to NEPA. In turn, such groups have been instrumental in lobbying for ever more stringent laws and in initiating environmental litigation.

Although traditionally a fairly powerless government clientele, welfare recipients acquired the status of an interest group in the mid-1960s through associations such as the National Welfare Rights Organization (NWRO). Gaining special-interest stature nearly 30 years after the inception of the federal cash public assistance program, NWRO and similar groups were themselves the offshoots of local "War on Poverty" activities. Relatively short-lived as a potent political force, welfare rights groups nonetheless frequently helped to expand program activities by informing poor non-recipients of available services and recipients of maximum rights and benefits under the law. In a few cases, the activities of such groups indeed led to benefit increases.[16] Perhaps even more important, these resultant welfare interests often played the classic "veto group" role. This was most evidently the case in NWRO's "Zap FAP" campaign, a successful effort aimed at thwarting enactment of the Nixon Family Assistance Plan.

Still another example of the resultant interest was found in higher-education policymaking. The "federal" orientation among higher-education institutions and associations largely originated in answer to the new federal programs of "The Great Society," gaining additional impetus as the financial problems of higher education became increasingly serious during the late 1960s. Hence, far from being responsible for most major programs, the higher-education lobby developed, to a considerable extent, in response to them.

Interest Groups and the "Spiral Effect"

Closely related to the concept of the resultant interest is the notion of a "spiral effect" in public policymaking. First described by political economists James M. Buchanan and Gordon Tulloch, the "spiral effect" is said to occur when

. . . other functional or interest groups, observing the success of the first, will now find it profitable to invest resources (funds) in political organization. The pressure group, as such, will rapidly become a part of the political decision-making process. Moreover, because of the activities of such groups, the range and extent of collective action will tend to be increased. As more and more groups come to recognize the advantages to be secured by special political dispensation, this organizational process will continue. The ultimate "equilibrium" will be reached only when all groups have become fully organized.[17]

Over time, federal area-development aid has produced just such a spiral effect. Hence, the original area-development law, the ARA, was regarded as "sectional" legislation. Despite its early demise, the ARA did succeed in creating demand for development fund jurisdictions. As a result, by 1979, ARA's successor, the Economic Development Administration (EDA), eventually encompassed 84.5 percent of the nation's population in its 2,230 designated areas.

This substantial accumulation of program constituency was accomplished through a series of liberalizing amendments which, in a little over a decade, reduced the minimum size of redevelopment areas from 250,000 to 25,000; redefined the status of recipient jurisdictions from "economically distressed communities" to "urban and rural areas . . . where long term economic deterioration has occurred or is taking place"; and added programs for economic recovery aid in disaster areas, adjustment assistance for areas experiencing structural economic dislocations, and emergency assistance to areas with unusually high unemployment rates. Thus EDA has probably ensured its survival by responding to nearly every conceivable group claim.

The Interest as Instigator

All the foregoing is not to suggest that interest groups never act in a policy-initiation capacity. Nor is it always clear just who the actual policy initiator is. The so-called issue network of congressional committees and their staffs, affected interests, and bureau and agency administrators at times obscures legislative authorship.[18] Hence, in what has been called the congressional phase of elementary and secondary education policy, lasting from 1870 to around 1960, "the actions Congress would be likely to take . . . were closely tied to what [a variety of] groups would accept or reject in any proposed bill."[19]

By far, the most vivid instance of interest-group initiative (or special-interest policy entrepreneurship) found in the ACIR case studies was that of federal aid to libraries and the force behind that aid, the American Library

Association (ALA). While not a special-interest powerhouse, the ALA excelled at a kind of classic coalition-building. Naturally, some of those included in the alliance for library aid were the specialized library organizations, such as the Association of Research Libraries and the Medical Library Association. Not unexpectedly, the education lobby was also an invaluable source of active endorsement, and the publishing industry lent at least tacit support. However, ALA's real strength, and the key to its victories, was in enlisting group support from organizations whose manifest connection with libraries was tenuous to say the least. Thus the Library Services Act, which aided rural libraries, was supported by farm organizations, and the 1977 renewal of the Library Services and Construction Act, which authorized funding for urban libraries, was supported by a variety of urban groups.

The Presidential Policy Role

If the case studies revealed a surprising amount of congressional activism, they also showed a surprising lack of protracted presidential involvement in the policy process. This partly stems from the President's routine policy role, from his immense visibility, and from the high expectations that surround and at times overwhelm the modern Presidency. The President's "star" status may lead to a distortion of his role, attributing to him more interest in or knowledge of a particular issue than he actually possesses. However, at times and often over the "biggest" issues, no single actor has loomed larger.

The President as Grand Policy Entrepreneur

Perhaps the most obvious and certainly the most dramatic case of presidential entrepreneurship occurred in the mid-1930s with the inception, legislative management, and passage of the Social Security Act. Truly an omnibus bill, the act created the current system of nationwide old-age insurance, three programs of categorical cash public assistance, unemployment insurance, and several programs of social and health services.

Originally, the Social Security Act was the product of the Committee on Economic Security. The committee was presidentially chosen, and while members and staff were charged with studying and making recommendations on all aspects of economic security, their primary concerns reflected those of President Roosevelt. Thus the lion's share of time and effort was spent on the problems of unemployment and old-age insurance. Despite his overwhelming preoccupation with these facets of economic security, Roosevelt insisted on presenting Congress with an omnibus bill encompassing insurance, public assistance, and social services. Despite a number of legislative roadblocks and a certain amount of congressional tunnel vision over the question of old-age assistance, he would accept nothing less from Congress than passage of every portion of his bill.[20] The success of Roosevelt's "all or nothing" entrepreneurial strategy is evident still in the existing social security, unemployment insurance, and cash public assistance system. In 1979, they accounted for an estimated $125 billion in federal outlays alone.[21]

The other outstanding example of the grand policy entrepreneur was found in the person of Lyndon Johnson and his sponsorship of the "War on Poverty." Like Roosevelt, Johnson transmitted a set of specific policy themes to a task force—in this instance, "poverty" rather than "economic security." And like Roosevelt, Johnson excelled at legislative management. In fact, James L. Sundquist has noted that Johnson's sponsorship of the Economic Opportunity Act of 1964 was "the most extreme case of legislative initiative by the President almost to the exclusion of Congress. . . ."[22] With the proper confluence of personality, legislative savvy, emotional interest, and a receptive public, press, and political climate, the Presidency showed itself to be a most powerful entrepreneurial tool. Such a fortuitous confluence, however, is quite rare.

The President as Dispassionate Promoter

There is a sense in which the Presidency may act as an agent of programmatic inception. The visibility, the expectations, and the centrality of the office may result in attributing to the President more interest in or knowledge of a given problem than actually is the case. Hence the legislative success of policies has often turned on a half-hearted or dispassionate presidential endorsement.

A notable example of this sort of presidential promotion is found in the area of fire protection. Early in 1967, President Johnson delivered his Consumer Protection Message to Congress, calling on the legislators to "improve our shameful record of losses of life and property through fires" and recommending the Fire Safety Act of 1967. Enmeshed as it was in a myriad of recommendations, the endorsement did not attract much public attention, but the fact that the President had spoken did give impetus and credibility to those working for federal assistance. Furthermore, it ensured consideration of fire legislation in Congress.

Obviously, in 1967, federal aid for local fire protection was not foremost among the many grave problems or even secondary issues facing the President. Yet, whether through the Assistant Secretary of Commerce for Science and Technology or through the possible intercession of Vice-President Humphrey, fire protection found its way into the presidential message, and eventually, fire-protection aid found its way into the array of federal programmatic endeavors.

Dispassionate presidential endorsements are not limited to the relative minutiae among potential programs. Indeed, something as major as the Employment Act of 1946, the single most important step in the governmental "institutionalization" of Keynesian economic theories, warranted little more than passing presidential interest.

Although presidential leadership has been an important ingredient in the passage of much of the New Deal social and economic legislation, this was not the case with the Employment Act. In fact, even the lukewarm support proffered initially by Roosevelt was probably due more to Republican opponent Thomas E. Dewey's endorsement of full employment than to any real presidential commitment. Moreover, despite the fact that President Truman tried to play a more forceful role, his promotional efforts merely succeeded in securing the bill's place on the legislative agenda. Thereafter, the formation, scope, and passage of the act proceeded according to congressional design.

The President as Restrainer

If Presidents tend to be enamored of costly, large-scale projects such as Social Security and the "War on Poverty," there is a conflicting presidential role that places them squarely in the forefront of budgetary restraint. The President, guiding and guided by the Office of Management and Budget (OMB), is the country's chief budgeteer, and promising to balance the nation's budget has long been a part of the standard candidate lexicon. In addition, Presidents attempt to play another sort of restraining role: that of restrainer of organizational and programmatic bloat. Thus, along with *low costs,* the rhetoric of the Presidency includes *efficiency* and *no waste.* In both these restraining roles, budgetary and institutional, Presidents generally have been less than successful.

One of the most lucid examples of the impotence of presidential restraint or reform efforts is provided in the area of welfare. The federal public-assistance role was presidentially initiated between 1933 and 1935, but since that time, Presidents have attempted in three distinct, reformist ways to regain a welfare role. In all three ways, they have been unsuccessful.

Beginning with the Truman administration, Presidents have attempted to curb welfare spending by asking Congress to hold the line on the federal share of benefits.[23] Congress, in turn, generally has responded to such presidential requests by increasing benefits or the federal share in benefits, or both.

Second, Presidents Kennedy and Johnson sought to get a handle on welfare by circumventing the congressional public-assistance system.

Heeding the clarion call of social-welfare workers, they sought to eliminate the welfare clientele through social rehabilitative services. The programs were largely unsuccessful; the number of clientele grew.

Finally, Presidents Nixon and Carter sought to reform welfare through federalization, guaranteed uniform incomes, and program consolidation. Thus far, the bulk of cash public assistance, AFDC, has proven resistant to all but the most incremental measures passing for reform.

In aid to elementary, secondary, and higher education, Presidents have tried with notable lack of success to control seemingly inevitable program growth and financial expansion. As early as 1966, President Johnson proposed a 50 percent cut in the popular impact-aid portion of his own Elementary and Secondary Education Act. Far from winning the battle, Johnson's economy effort resulted in a continuation of full federal funding for the program, overall Senate education authorizations amounting to almost $1 billion above his request, and a $700 million increase in the final legislation. Moreover, this trend continued under Nixon, when in 1969, the administration's proposed $450 million reduction in the education budget was met in Congress with a $1 billion increase.

A similar pattern emerged in higher education under President Nixon. In 1971, the administration submitted to Congress a proposal that required that aid to students be more strictly targeted on the basis of need and that limited total aid to these students to $1,400 per year. In addition, more emphasis was to be placed on loans than grants, and higher-education categoricals were to be consolidated into a National Foundation for Higher Education.

Needless to say, the proposals were roundly criticized in Congress from all sides—for their limited budget, heavy reliance on loans, and inattention to the needs of hard-pressed schools and middle-class students. As a result, the bill received little support from either side of the aisle in Congress and represented another resounding education defeat for the Nixon Presidency.

In recent years, much has come to be expected of government. But if much is expected of government in general, more is expected of its most visible officer, the President. He is expected at once to be the purveyor of new panacean policies and of a tight, no-growth budget, to innovate while holding the nation firmly to its traditions, and to provide programmatic latitude while keeping tight reins on the bureaucracy. It is not at all surprising that these contradictory and semicelestial expectations have seldom been realized in practice.

Although in certain expansionary efforts Presidents have had notable successes, they have exhibited an equally notable tendency toward failure in their companion restraint role. Moreover, any number of assumed presidential "successes" have occurred in areas in which the President's interest was transitory at best, in which he payed effective lip service to a "winning" program or policy. The presidential role has been ambivalent, at times enigmatic, and in its triple functional designations of entrepreneur, promoter, and restrainer, perhaps overly ambitious.

The Bureaucratic Policy Role

Even more surprisingly than with the President, the federal bureaucracy was found in the case studies to have had a much less substantial role in the inception of government policy than much of the literature would suggest.[24] As always, however, the standard caveat applies: a less substantial role than expected should not imply no role at all. Obviously, just as Congress and Presidents automatically play a policy role, so some segment of the bureaucracy must always be charged with carrying out the law. Thereafter, the latitude afforded to the bureaucrats in question is often dependent on the type of law and, even more important, the degree of specificity in the legislative language. Moreover, within the realm of long-standing policy areas, bureaucrats may seek to become advocates for additional (or second-generation) programs. Such activity, classified as jurisdictional expansion or empire-building, has traditionally been the subject of much public-administration literature—often to the point where the reader might assume that bureaucrats are usually engaged in a byzantine atmosphere of power accumulation. Yet, while the case studies did include a few examples that might loosely be classified as bureaucratic jurisdictional expansion, this type appeared neither frequently nor clearly enough to attribute to them a conscious and consistent effort toward power aggregation.

The Bureaucracy and Regulatory Law

Particularly in the realm of regulatory law, the congressional tendency has been increasingly to write and pass broad, symbolic legislation without much substantive content. It falls then to an administrative agency to define the scope and intent of the law. Such broad delegation of power has been called, by Theodore J. Lowi, "policy without law," a congressional habit that "has wrapped public policy in shrouds of illegitimacy and ineffectiveness."[25] It is within the realm of such regulatory delegation that the potential for a bureaucratic effect on policy development has been the greatest.

One of the broadest regulatory delegations found in the case studies occurred with the enactment of the National Environmental Policy Act (NEPA) in 1969. The Council on Environmental Quality (CEQ) was instructed to develop policies in accordance with the purposes of NEPA and was charged with evaluating other federal programs in order to determine if their activities were contributing to "the purposes of [the] Act:"

To declare a national policy which will encourage productive and enjoyable harmony between man and his environment; to promote efforts which will prevent or eliminate damage to the environment and biosphere and stimulate the health and welfare of man; to enrich the understanding of the ecological systems and natural resources important to the Nation; and to establish a Council on Environmental Quality.[26]

Unfortunately, the "purposes" of the act were so sweeping, philosophical, and symbolic as to force CEQ into the role of legislative interpreter prior to developing policies on enforcement mechanisms. Under such circumstances, the CEQ conceivably could have amassed a tremendous amount of power and jurisdictional latitude. The fact that it ultimately chose for itself a relatively limited role, leaving the more substantive environmental tasks to the Environmental Protection Agency (EPA), created 1 year later through Presidential reorganization, indicates that the potential for bureaucratic power under broad regulatory grants often remains exactly that.

A different characterization of the bureaucracy and its potential under more or less symbolic congressional regulatory enactments is provided in the area of higher education, particularly Title IX of the Education Amendments of 1972, which prohibits sex discrimination in educational institutions. As was clearly the case 3 years earlier with NEPA, the winning congressional vote was based almost entirely on vague and lofty principles rather than on any understanding of legal implications. As a result, "Congress made no attempt to provide a clear and complete definition of what constituted sex discrimination in education,"[27] and an ill-experienced and virtually unguided Office of Civil Rights (OCR) was compelled to draft the regulations, a process that took an arduous 3 years.

In July 1975, the final regulations of Title IX took effect. They were far-reaching and prompted vociferous controversy. Yet, considering their long and difficult development, the regulations cannot be said to have evolved without ample opportunity for oversight. Both the President and Congress could have intervened to reject or alter the regulations, since the law required unusual presidential and congressional clearance procedures prior to implementation. All this potential oversight resulted only in very limited revisions. Hence, in this case, far from searching after a power role, the bureaucracy had a substantial amount of power thrust upon it.

The Bureaucracy and Functional Resistance

As previously noted, the case studies found few (if any true) instances of bureaucratic empire-building. In fact, much clearer and more notable were the instances of bureaucratic resistance to the accumulation of new and additional responsibilities.

Thus, although the possibility of some form of federal air-pollution enforcement procedure had been discussed throughout much of the 1950s, the actual realization of even the most benign enforcement procedures was successfully resisted until 1963. Significantly, the bulk of this resistance came from the Public Health Service (PHS), the very agency that would have gained jurisdictionally from the new procedures.

In 1975, in the field of welfare, bureaucratic resistance again managed to thwart change. Unwilling to administer a new negative income tax, or Income Supplement Plan (ISP) as the proposal was dubbed under the Ford administration, then Secretary of HEW Caspar Weinberger sought to have the potential new welfare system run by the Internal Revenue Service (IRS). An indication of Treasury's willingness to allow agency expansion was duly noted by officials of the Department in their claim that there would be "nothing but trouble for the department and the IRS if the revenue collection agency were to be assigned the job of running ISP."[28]

The Bureaucracy and Program Initiation

In the realm of program initiation, the bureaucratic role may be described as sporadic and largely secondary. In the cases studied, bureaucratic policy entrepreneurs were relatively infrequent actors and generally entered the initiation process at the behest of some other actor, usually the President. Certainly, this occurred in the previously mentioned instances of presidential grand policy entrepreneurship, the Social Security Act and the "War on Poverty" effort. In both cases, the President ordered the bureaucracy to create far-reaching legislation based on specific presidential guidelines. Although in each case the bureaucratic role or effect was profound, it was primarily an extension of presidential entrepreneurship. In like manner, Department of Health, Education and Welfare (HEW) influence on the development of ESEA and the Department of Agriculture's (USDA) importance in pushing for food stamp legislation reflected the priorities of Presidents Johnson and Kennedy respectively.

In fact, in only one program that the commission studied, the rural community fire program, did a segment of the bureaucracy manifestly act as a primary policy entrepreneur. Hence, empire-building on the part of the U.S. Forest Service may have been a factor in the efforts of the agency to broaden its activities, and some feel that the service engaged in a "power grab." Equally plausible is the theory that the Forest Service recognized a need and moved to fill it. Whatever the case, the Forest Service clearly acted as the initiator, chief promoter, and prime mover behind the federal role in rural fire protection.

The Judicial Policy Role

Determining the political impact of the "nonpolitical" branch of government has proven to be no mean feat for any number of analysts. The judiciary does not, in a technical or visible sense, create or pass laws; it has no tangible means of execution or implementation, and although the activity is not unheard of among "actively concerned" jurists, lobbying on the part of judges is considered to be somewhat unethical. At least it is seldom noted in legislative histories.

The Court may, of course, rule on the legitimacy of narrow statutory language or on the degree to which implementation matches congressional intent. In each way it contributes to the shape and functional scope of government. But in a much larger sense, one often underlying rather than specifically stated in the case studies, the Court may send signals to the other branches and levels of government, interested groups, and the citizenry at large of just what is or what is not legally, and even morally and politically, acceptable. Since 1937 and the Roosevelt Court battle, Congress has been relatively unconstrained in its interpretation of *necessary and proper* of what constitutes legitimate spending for the general welfare, and what activities, intrastate as well interstate, are justifiable national concerns under the interstate commerce clause.[29] Moreover, since the early 1920s, the Court has consistently given its approval to the accomplishment of national purposes through conditional grants-in-aid.[30] All these judicial "green lights" offered to Congress the legal mechanisms for expanding the federal functional role.

Yet, in spite of the fact that the federal government possessed the legal authority and means for expansion, the prevailing political climate or mood prevented the widespread use of them. Despite the cost and importance of the New Deal programs, the quantity and types of functions into which the national government was willing to delve remained relatively small into the 1960s, when a number of factors began to erode the existing political constraints. Having been a leader in offering the legal mechanisms for expansion just a few decades before, the Court was also chief among those setting the political *mood* for expansion.

Thus, from the mid to late 1950s and continuing through the 1970s, what has come to be known as "judicial activism" worked both directly and circuitously to enlarge and legitimize the number and types of functions under Congress' substantial spending and commerce powers and under the First and Fourteenth Amendments. Moreover, the judicial philosophy pervading one area of constitutional concern, for example, discrimination, had the effect of broadening and deepening federal involvement in a discrete statutory function. An excellent case study lies in the realm of elementary and secondary education.

Several factors have been at work in the expansion of the Court's—and thus the federal government's—role in education. First, of course, is the process of constitutional interpretation. The Constitution itself is frequently vague, requiring that the Court give meaning to such expressions as "equal protection of the laws." New interpretations have expanded the judicial role in several ways. Hence, development of the First Amendment guarantees has been part of the twentieth-century trend of applying the Bill of Rights to state practices in contrast to earlier interpretations. In addition, the Court has increased its role of defending the rights of "discrete and insular minorities" that may not be protected in the majoritarian democratic process.

Another aspect of judicial expansion has been the institutional process of Court involvement. This can be seen in the race-discrimination cases. Implementation of the *Brown* decision appeared to be a moderate process of "all deliberate speed."[31] Yet, such eminent observers as Archibald Cox argue that it entailed a new dimension of judicial enforcement.[32] Rather than simply prohibiting a certain practice, it established "affirmative duties" on the part of the defendant jurisdiction, since the latter had to institute specific reforms in order to comply with the law.[33] A lack of compliance could produce increasingly detailed instructions on conformity, urged by the plaintiff. An unexpected degree of judicial involvement in the administration of a school could and did evolve from the process of enforcement.

A third factor increasing education litigation has been the effect of other governmental programs. In other words, judicial activity sets a political tone that may act to fan the flames of congressional activity, which in turn produces more judicial activity. Thus federal laws such as title IX and the Civil Rights Act (themselves inspired partly by judicial civil rights rulings) have required judicial interpretation.

To summarize, the Court has been a powerful, if often circuitous, instrument of government growth and deepening federal intergovernmental involvement. Over time, it has provided Congress with the mechanisms for pursuing growth, the climate for enacting growth, and the legal interpretations for implementing growth. Moreover, it has served both as an arena for, and sometimes a source of, interest groups. The "nonpolitical" branch of government, then, has been a potent force in forming the political shape of the nation.

Policymaking and the External Actor

Certain "actors"—public opinion, elections political parties, and the press—that have an effect on the absolute size, breadth, and depth of the federal government are endowed with traits that distinguish them from the inside players reviewed earlier. First, they all act indirectly on the functional scope of government. That is, they do not legislate, administer, legally sanction, or lobby for particular policies. Although intrinsically tied to government, they are government outsiders.

They are less visible in an individual sense and thus more difficult to personify than the inside player. The roles and rationales of a particular representative, President, cabinet member, Chief Justice, or lobbyist are much easier to analyze than those of Jane Q. Public.

Finally, each of these "external" actors, in some way, may be alleged to measure or organize popular desires. This characteristic is the most significant of all, for a common and certainly enduring complaint asserts that popularly elected officials, particularly members of Congress, are not responsive to the people they claim to represent.

Yet, even a brief review of the activities of the inside players, and especially Congress, would seem to indicate that they respond often, to everyone, and with the energy of one possessed. The very quantity and variety of legislation that has emanated from Capitol Hill at least since the mid-1960s suggests that *hyper*responsiveness is the rule and *hypo*responsiveness, the exception.

Hence, responsiveness per se is not the problem. Rather, two questions arise: To what is government responding? And how accountable has it been following the initial response? In other words, have the people gotten what they want? The question "To what is government responding?" will be explored in the following section.

The Role of Public Opinion and Elections

Public opinion is measured in a number of ways. In a representative democracy, of course, elections are the traditional orderly and legally prescribed means of expressing popular desires or opinions. Yet, *vox populi* is not always orderly, not always willing to express itself only biennially, and not always able to encourage the adoption of discrete policy positions at the ballot box. Hence, popular sentiment may be expressed through opinion polls, through any number of citizen-participation devices, through direct correspondence or contact with elected officials, or in its most extreme form short of revolution, through popular demonstration.[34]

In the era of Proposition 13, when the public appears to be demanding less government, it has been noted that *less government* does not necessarily mean fewer or smaller programs. Rather, *less government* seems to mean, on the one level, a concrete desire for less burdensome taxes and on another, perhaps more profound level, a deep-seated American ideological commitment to the Jeffersonian notion of limited government, or the "negative liberal state."

Americans have increasingly displayed since the New Deal a striking ambivalence toward the role of the modern state. That is, we tend to consent to the growth of government in a discrete programmatic sense, but disdain the growth of government in a broad philosophic sense. Remarking on this simultaneous attraction toward and repulsion from government as early as 1964, public-opinion experts Lloyd Free and Hadley Cantril concluded that most Americans could be described as "operational liberals" and "ideological conservatives." Hence, many who continue to identify with the negative liberal state in the abstract fully support government activism in specific instances.[35] Nowhere is this American paradox seen more clearly than in public-opinion polls.

Not unexpectedly, among the case-study examples, the most dramatic instance of public-opinion support for strong federal activism was found in the environment. Between 1969 and 1971, according to the Opinion Research Corporation, the environment jumped from being last among a series of problems with which the public was concerned to second among those problems.[36] Moreover, the environment, along with health, was found by the National Opinion Research Center in 1973 to be second only to crime among federal program areas in which the public felt the federal government was spending "too little."[37] The public appeared to be providing the federal government with a mandate to continue to move full speed ahead on environmental matters often, critics allege, to the point where it became wrongfully preemptive or coercive of state actions.

Over time, public-opinion polls have offered at least vague support for federal spending programs in education, unemployment, and even welfare, although recently such support has been on the decline for welfare.[38] Thus, through polls the public favors a federal-program presence. Although often amorphous or highly generalized, such articulation of support may be viewed as one more "green light" for federal expansion.

Elections have been an even more generalized though certainly more legitimate mechanism than public-opinion polls for public expression of support for or opposition to federal activism. Of course, at the most fundamental level, elections are the source of congressional entrepreneurs. For our purposes, the importance of elections lies in their real or perceived outcome as mandates and their functions as an ex post facto means of approval. In this capacity, election results may be said to have contributed to the increasing amount of federal activity.

Two elections have been extremely important in both respects. In 1936 and 1964, the public was perceived not only to be providing Presidents Roosevelt and Johnson and the Democratic Congresses with resounding approval of past activist policies but with mandates for additional activism. Moreover, three other elections also have been significant. The 1932 and 1958 elections were perceived as mandates and the 1934 election was seen as an electoral ratification of past activity. Hence the way in which past

Presidents and Congresses have perceived election results has contributed to broad (as well as narrow) activist policies and consequently government growth.

Has the "popular will," then, contributed to the growth of the grant and regulatory systems? The answer, undoubtedly, is yes. In both 1932 and 1964, the President and Congress *perceived* a particular type of popular mandate and acted accordingly. Whether or not the perception was valid, policymakers thought they were responding appropriately. Moreover, despite its designation as the party of "big spenders" and "big government," the electorate has chosen Democratic Congresses for all but 4 of the past 50 years and has opted for five Democrats out of the last seven elected Presidents. Taking political note of these public preferences, the Republican Party generally has at least sustained and in recent history has sometimes expanded the grant and regulatory arenas.

Public opinion, too, as a polled and demonstrated commodity has expressed its approval of federal growth—operationally, if not ideologically. Generalized dissatisfaction with government more often than not fails to evince itself in specific dissatisfaction with individual government program endeavors. Moreover, to the most extreme and visible instance of "public opinion," the broad-based and vocal middle-class concern over environmental deterioration, Congress, as a political body, had little choice but to respond forcefully and rapidly. On still another level, as exemplified by food stamps, area development, and fire protection, specific members of Congress responded to constituent needs—precisely the function that members of Congress are supposed to perform.

The problem of government size in a functional sense was born of and nurtured on the perceptions of those who make policy—in their interpretations of and response to public signals. Yet, responsiveness in government, by almost anyone's yardstick, lies more in the realm of virtue than in that of vice. Hence the real failure, that failure which results in overload, super-marbleization, and excessive intrusiveness, lies elsewhere. It lies in how policymakers treat the signals, exhibiting responsible, publicly answerable development of those signals which benefit the larger society or segments of the society which the larger society has chosen to reject and filtering out those which benefit only parochial interests or which could be adequately handled elsewhere. That is a failure of accountability, a failure of *responsive* policymakers to be *responsible* policymakers.

The Policy Environment

Policy actors do not operate in a vacuum. Rather, they are forced constantly to respond not only to other actors (the repeated occurrence of which was detailed earlier, but also to the surrounding economic, social, international, technological, and demographic environments. Inasmuch as all these elements remain reasonably stable, policy might be expected to advance at a reasonably steady (or incremental) rate. Yet the outside environment is not always cooperative: the Soviet Union seldom consults with U.S. policymakers as to its plans for troop movements, nor can our own financial experts agree on the state of the economy even 1 or 2 months in advance. Occasionally then, both large and small instabilities in the environment must be dealt with, and the political responses to certain of these environmental instabilities have been critical in determining the shape and scope of modern government. For our purposes, such instabilities included both unanticipated *trends* and abrupt or unexpected *dislocations*.[39]

The term *dislocations* may encompass any number of critical events, from those which affect the society at large to those which affect only certain segments of the population. Those which are, at once, both extremely severe and affect the entire society would be expected to have the greatest impact on the "shapers" and consequently the shape of government. Needless to say, in the time frame of the case studies, the two most notable examples of this sort have been the Great Depression and World War II.

When the first symptom of the Great Depression, the stock market crash of 1929, occurred the vast majority of the American public perceived the national government as a vague and remote protector of their rights to "life, liberty, and property." Even at that, the popular expectation was not that Washington would guard against internal threats to property by untimely economic reversals; if any governments were expected to perform those tasks, they were the states and localities. Rather, the general perception of the national government was that of protector against broad foreign threats of those rights. At the dawn of the 1930s, ideological and operational perceptions were fairly consistent.

True, the electorate rejected conservative Herbert Hoover in 1932, but significantly not because he had not enacted large-scale federal programs. Instead, his defeat occurred because of a generalized dissatisfaction with his uninspired leadership in a time of crisis. Moreover, the man whom the public chose sounded, throughout the campaign, a more conservative, less government activist note than his opponent, prompting one commentator to remark that, "Given later developments, the campaign speeches often read like a giant misprint in which Roosevelt and Hoover speak each other's lines."[40]

Nor could it be alleged that once in office, Roosevelt initially adopted a strong expansionist philosophy. In a sense, the father of New Deal liberalism could only loosely be described as a New Deal liberal. Rather, Roosevelt was a pragmatist, who responded pragmatically, albeit with a vast expansion in the functional responsibilities of the federal government, to a profound economic dislocation. Hence the government response to the depression was a diverse series of massive new federal programs, both spending and regulatory, aimed at ensuring the present and future economic security of the nation as well as the individual. More important than their effect on the size of government, however, these New Deal programs began changing popular expectations regarding what the national government could and should do for its citizens.

The metamorphosis of "Dr. New Deal" into "Dr. Win-the-War," also went far in expanding the federal role. Normally, entry into a war can be expected to alter profoundly the revenue-producing and expenditure patterns of the central government fighting the war. After the war, the theory goes, such patterns fail to return to their pre-war levels.[41] America's role in World War II and its postwar economy bear this out, for the most important postwar economic decision was that the increased and expanded tax base generated by war could not be substantially reduced. Instead, resources formerly devoted to defense were switched to expanded domestic purposes.[42] Hence, in large part, the war effort removed from the federal government many previously existing fiscal constraints.

From a discrete programmatic perspective, other less profound dislocations, perhaps more aptly termed *surprises*, also have been instrumental in contributing to an increased national presence. The case studies contained two notable examples of such surprises.

One of the most dramatic events of the Cold War era was the launching in 1957 of the Soviet satellite, Sputnik. Thereafter, it became common wisdom that Americans suffered from a "knowledge gap," that educationally we had fallen dangerously behind our "arch-enemy."

In Congress and within the Eisenhower administration, such thinking ended a long-standing religious and racial stalemate over federal aid to education. Thus the legislation that became the National Defense Education Act (NDEA) was developed almost simultaneously by Senator Lister Hill and Representative Carl Elliot and the administration. Given the previous constitutional and social objections to federal aid to education, its passage, less than 1 year after Sputnik, was nothing short of phenomenal. This Cold War phenomenon gave powerful new impetus to federal involvement in the field of education.

Just a decade after Sputnik, another more immediate and more tragic surprise confronted the United States. In 1967, the public and policymakers alike watched in horror as riots engulfed entire portions of major cities in the flames of frustration and shattered hopes. The impact was profound on many levels. Yet, for our purposes (and on a much smaller level), the fires resulting from the riots drew attention to the occupational hazards of fire fighting and created an environment in Congress favorable to a federal role in local fire activities, a role that came to fruition the following year.

A final type of dislocation, the discovery of what might be termed a *segmented dislocation* within a period of general normalcy also has contributed to the growth of the federal government. The results of one dramatic and telling discovery is exemplified by the "War on Poverty." Thus, Michael Harrington's *The Other America* and John Kenneth Gailbraith's *The Affluent Society* detailed the existence of previously ignored poverty in a nation which, on the whole, was more prosperous than ever before. The books apparently had an enormous impact on President Kennedy, whose subsequent determintion to inaugurate a poverty program was launched by his successor.

Conclusions

Policy by grants and regulations is habit-forming and may be hazardous to the health of the polity. In the world of policy entrepreneurs no longer disciplined by constitutional, political, or institutional constraints, individual responsiveness to almost any conceivable stimulus, whether large, small, important, trivial, or of national or local interest, is the eventual outcome. Such responsiveness finds convenient outlet in the constant enactment of narrow grants and broad, lofty regulatory language, the "cheap" ways of being active. A small grant program aimed at a few jurisdictions is a drop in the budgetary bucket, and price tags are not attached to ideals.

While policy entrepreneurs may dominate this world, they are not its only occupants. Programs beget resultant interests that soon come to depend on existing policy and demand increasing benefits. Programs that affect a few jurisdictions seldom remain politically viable and eventually must spread or flounder. As if straight out of Lewis Carroll's Wonderland, targeting becomes a synonym for its own antonym.

So too, abstract ideals eventually are translated into concrete rules, and while ideals are priceless, aggregated rules can be very costly indeed. Nor do such costs merely include the fiscal burdens that accrue to regulator as well as regulated. Rather, in the cases of both grants and regulations, there also exist the enormous costs associated with the almost unintelligible complexity and confusion that result from the extreme intergovernmentalization of nearly every public endeavor. In the end, these may be the most important and expensive costs attached to the "cheap" ways of being active.

Notes

1. The idea of intergovernmental relations resembling a "marble cake" was conceived by the late Morton Grodzins. See, for example, Mor-

ton Grodzins, *The American System* (Chicago: Rand McNally, 1966), pp. 7-10.

2. The highwater mark in federal civilian employment was reached in the mid-1940s with over 3.5 million civilians employed. That number declined drastically following the war, increased somewhat during the Korean war, and decreased again until the early 1960s. Employment once more peaked at just over 3 million in the late 1960s. Today, federal civilian employment, including approximately 600,000 postal workers, stands at about 2.8 million. Not only has employment decreased absolutely, it has decreased even more sharply in relative terms: in terms of employment per thousand population, in terms of employees per $1 million of outlays, and in terms of total (federal, state, local) government labor force. See "Indicators of Federal Growth," Chapter 2, Volume I of Advisory Commission on Intergovernmental Relations, *The Federal Role in the Federal System* (1980).

3. While no one knows how much mandates cost state and local governments, the most thorough study of the subject to date has concluded that "the concern of local government officials about the burden that mandating is placing on their local resources is justified." Catherine H. Lovell et al., *Federal and State Mandating on Local Governments: An Exploration of Issues and Impacts,* Final Report to the National Science Foundation (Riverside, Calif.: Univ. of California Press, 1979), p. 169.

4. Despite the fact that states and localities have begun increasingly to complain about the practical coercive effect of many grant conditions, for the past 57 years the courts have ruled that grants are voluntary agreements and therefore conditions attached are not coercive.

5. For two of the best studies of congressional policymaking, see Gary Orfield, *Congressional Power: Congress and Social Change* (New York: Harcourt, Brace, Jovanovich, 1975); and Randall B. Ripley, *Congress: Process and Policy* (New York: Norton, 1975).

6. Advisory Commission on Intergovernmental Relations, *Categorical Grants: Their Role and Design* (A-52) (Washington: USGPO, 1977), p. 65.

7. Ibid.

8. Ibid., pp. 63-64.

9. Ibid., p. 65.

10. "Personal Privacy in an Information Society: The Report of the Privacy Protection Study Commission," reprinted in the U.S. House of Representatives, *Hearings before the Subcommittee on Elementary, Secondary, and Vocational Education of the Committee on Education and Labor on H.R. 15, Part 9: Family Educational Rights and Privacy Act of 1974,* 95th Congress, 1st Sess., 1977, pp. 130-131.

11. Charles O. Jones has dubbed this sort of policy escalation, "specu-

lative augmentation." Hence, with regard to the Clean Air Act of 1970, Jones notes that "whereas we normally think of formulations preceding majority-building in the policy process and identify each step with the executive and legislative, respectively, in 1970 a majority seemingly awaited unspecified strong action. Thus, instead of a majority having to be established for a policy, a policy had to be constructed for a majority. Much of that occurred within Congress as proposals escalated toward various actors' perceptions of what was necessary to meet public demands." Charles O. Jones, *Clean Air: The Policies and Politics of Pollution Control* (Pittsburgh: Univ. of Pittsburgh Press, 1975), p. 176.

12. This has been called the "withering away fallacy." Gilbert Steiner, *Social Insecurity: The Politics of Welfare* (Chicago: Rand McNally, 1966), pp. 18–47.

13. *Congressional Record,* vol. 125, no. 164, 96th Congress, 1st Sess., 1979, pp. H11024–H11124.

14. While we have termed this phenomenon *resultant interests,* another recent study defines them as "imputed interests." Guy C. Colarulli and Bruce F. Berg, "Imputed Interests: An Impact of Policy," paper prepared for delivery at the 1979 Annual Meeting of the American Political Science Association.

15. As noted previously, one of the reasons that Congress prefers the narrow intergovernmental program approach to policymaking is the accessibility to interest groups of committees and subcommittees. Moreover, interest groups themselves tend to favor the same approach. Hence, according to Phillip Monypenny, "It can be asserted . . . that politically speaking, federal aid programs are the outcome of a loose coalition which resorts to a mixed federal-state program because it is not strong enough in individual states to secure its program, and because it is not united enough to achieve a wholly federal program against the opposition which a specific program would engender." Viewed from that perspective, "the grant-in-aid programs make sense." Phillip Monypenny, "Federal Grants-In-Aid to State Governments: A Political Analysis," *National Tax Journal* 13 (March 1960):15.

16. Joe R. Feagin, *Subordinating the Poor: Welfare and American Beliefs* (Englewood Cliffs, N.J., Prentice-Hall, 1975), p. 81.

17. James M. Buchanan and Gordon Tulloch, *The Calculus of Consent: Logical Foundations of Constitutional Democracy* (Ann Arbor, Mich.: Univ. of Michigan Press, 1965), pp. 287–288.

18. For a discussion of the "issue network," see H. Brinton Milward, "Policy Entrepreneurship and Bureaucratic Demand Creation," in Helen M. Ingram and Dean E. Mann (eds.), *Why Policies Succeed or Fail* (Beverly Hills, Calif.: Sage, 1980), p. 261.

19. Eugene Eidenberg and Roy Morey, *An Act of Congress* (New York, Norton, 1969), p. 60.

20. One of the best accounts of the developmental stage of social security has been provided by the Executive Director of the Committee on Economic Security, Edwin E. Witte. Edwin E. Witte, *The Development of the Social Security Act* (Madison, Wisc.: Univ. of Wisconsin Press, 1962). Another good history is proffered by one of the first three members of the Social Security Board and its second chairman, Arthur J. Altmeyer. Arthur J. Altmeyer, *The Formative Years of Social Security* (Madison, Wisc.: Univ. of Wisconsin Press, 1966). Finally, for an excellent contemporary study of the subject, see Martha Derthick, *Policymaking for Social Security* (Washington: Brookings Institution, 1979).

21. Executive Office of the President, Office of Management and Budget, *The Budget of the United States Goverment, 1980* (Washington: USGPO, 1979), pp. 250–251. Roosevelt's "pet program," the old-age, survivor's, and disability program (OASDI, or popularly, Social Security) is, itself, the largest single item in the federal budget, accounting for an estimated $102.3 billion in 1979 outlays. Executive Office of the President, Office of Management and Budget, *The United States Budget in Brief* (Washington: USGPO, 1979), p. 54.

22. James L. Sundquist, *Politics and Policy* (Washington: Brookings Institution, 1968), p. 493.

23. In fact, a certain amount of presidential despair over rising welfare costs was noted as early as 1939 when, in response to a potential increase, President Roosevelt remarked, "Not one nickle more, not one solitary nickle. Once you get off the 50–50 matching basis, the sky's the limit, and before you know it, we'll be paying the whole bill." Quoted in Altmeyer, *The Formative Years of Social Security,* p. 112.

24. As an example, see a number of articles in Francis E. Rourke (ed.), *Bureaucratic Power in National Politics,* 2d ed. (Boston: Little, Brown, 1972).

25. Theodore J. Lowi, *The End of Liberalism* (New York: Norton, 1969), pp. 126–127.

26. The National Environmental Policy Act, Pub. L. 91–90, 83 Stat. 852, January 1, 1970.

27. Andrew Fishel and Janice Pottker, *National Politics and Sex Discrimination in Education* (Lexington, Mass.: Lexington Books, D.C. Heath, 1977), p. 132.

28. John J. Iglehart, "HEW Wants Welfare Programs Replaced by Negative Income Tax," *National Journal Reports* 6 (42):1564.

29. The most notable exception occurred in National League of Cities v. Usery, 426 U.S. 833 (1976).

30. Massachusetts v. Mellon (Frothingham v. Mellon), 262 U.S. 447 (1923); for a more complete explanation, see Thomas J. Madden, "The Law of Federal Grants," paper prepared for Advisory Commission on Intergovernmental Relation's Conference on Grant Law, Washington, D.C., December 12, 1979.

31. Brown v. Board of Education of Topeka, Kansas, 347 U.S. 483 (1954).

32. Archibald Cox, *The Role of the Supreme Court in American Government* (New York: Oxford Univ. Press, 1976), p. 77.

33. Lau v. Nichols, 414 U.S. 563 (1974).

34. Citizen-participation devices such as procedures for public comment at the drafting or implementation phase of legislation did not figure heavily in any of the case-study programs. However, for a thorough analysis of citizen participation, see ACIR, *Citizen Participation in the American Federal System* (A–73) (Washington: USGPO, 1980). In discrete instances, however, both correspondence and demonstrations have had a profound effect on the deepening of federal program involvement. Hence, a letter-writing campaign spurred the expansion of the Food Stamp Program in the late 1960s, while Earth Day 1970 acted as a powerful catalyst for the environmental legislation of the 1970s.

35. Lloyd Free and Hadley Cantril, *The Political Beliefs of Americans* (New York: Clarion Books, 1968), p. 32–37. For a fuller description of this phenomenon and its effects, see "Government UnLocked: Political Constraints on Federal Growth Since the 1930s," Vol. II, Chapter 3 of ACIR, *The Federal Role in the Federal System* (1980).

36. Opinion Research Corporation, "Public Opinion on Key Domestic Issues," Princeton, N.J., May 1971, p. 17 (mimeographed). See also, John C. Whitaker, *Striking a Balance: Environment and Natural Resources Policy in the Nixon-Ford Years* (Washington: American Enterprise Institute for Public Policy Research, 1976), p. 8.

37. National Opinion Research Center, "General Social Survey," in "What the Public Thinks," *Resources* 57 (January-March 1978):21.

38. In the two other case studies examined, libraries and fire protection, the question of federal involvement either has never been posed (as in fire protection) or was posed only once and in such a way as to make interpretation difficult (as in libraries.)

39. Space prevents an examination of economic, social, technological, ecological, and demographic trends. However, in the cases of environment, public assistance, unemployment, and education, one or more such trends did figure in deepening federal involvement. For a discussion, see ACIR, *The Federal Role in The Federal System* (1980).

40. Unnamed New Deal administrator quoted in William E. Leuchten-

burg, *Franklin D. Roosevelt and the New Deal* (New York: Harper and Row, 1963), p. 11.

41. For the basic study of this type, see Alan T. Peacock and Jack Wiseman, *The Growth of Public Expenditure in the United Kingdom* (Princeton, N.J.: Princeton Univ. Press, 1961).

42. For a thorough analysis of the breakdown of fiscal constraints on the federal government, see "Financing Federal Growth: Changing Aspects of Fiscal Constraints," Vol. II, Chapter 4 of ACIR, *The Federal Role in the Federal System* (1980).

Index

About the Contributors

David Beam is senior analyst with the Advisory Commission on Intergovernmental Relations. He is coauthor of *Analyzing State and Local Politics* and has written a number of special studies on federalism for ACIR. He is a coauthor of a multivolume study of the role of the national government in the federal system.

Cynthia Cates Colella is policy analyst with the Advisory Commission on Intergovernmental Relations. She is the author of "The Creation, Care, and Feeding of Leviathan" in *Intergovernmental Perspective* and is coauthor of a multivolume study of the role of the national government in the federal system.

Melvin J. Dubnick is associate professor of political science at the University of Kansas. He is the author of several articles on regulatory policy and coauthor of a forthcoming textbook entitled *Policy Analysis: A Problem Solving Approach.*

Alan R. Gitelson is associate professor of political science at Loyola University of Chicago. He is coauthor of "Political Stability and Urban Reform Club Activism" in *Polity* (1978) and has written widely on voting behavior and regulatory analysis.

Thomas H. Jones is professor of education at the University of Connecticut, Storrs. He has written widely on education policy and school costs, was a member of the President's Task Force on Education Costs, and has published in the *Journal of Education Finance.*

Joseph F. Zimmerman is professor of political science at the State University of New York at Albany. He is an official consultant to the U.S. Advisory Commission on Intergovernmental Relations and is the author of *State and Local Government* and coauthor of *The Politics of the Veto of Legislation in New York.*

About the Editor

Jerome J. Hanus received the B.A. from Seattle University, the M.A. from the University of Washington, and the Ph.D. from the University of Maryland. Dr. Hanus is professor of government at The American University where he specializes in constitutional law. He has published articles in a number of journals, including the *American Journal of Legal History* and the *American University Law Review*. Dr. Hanus was the British Petroleum Fellow in American Studies at the University of Dundee (1972–1973) and was Scholar in Residence with the Southern Growth Policies Board (1979–1980). This volume is an outgrowth of his work with the Board.

353.9
N277   Hanus, Jerome J.

            The nationalization of state

government